How to Win the Nobel Prize In Literature

A Handbook for the Would-be Laureate

How to Win the Nobel Prize In Literature
A Handbook for the Would-be Laureate

by

David Carter

Published by Hesperus Press Limited
28 Mortimer Street, London W1W 7RD
www.hesperuspress.com

First published by Hesperus Press Limited, 2012
Copyright © David Carter, 2012

The right of David Carter to be identified as the Author of the Work
has been asserted by him in accordance with the Copyright, Designs
and Patent Act 1988.

Designed and typeset by Fraser Muggeridge studio
Printed in Jordan by Jordan National Press

ISBN: 978-1-84391-374-0

Contents

In fond memory of
Dennis Burton,
a man of science and lover of literature.

Introduction

If anyone is foolish enough to set him- or herself the goal of winning the Nobel Prize in Literature, then this book will provide some insight into the trials, tribulations and the pitfalls likely to be encountered in pursuit of that dream. The reader will also find an account of the qualities that have made for a successful laureate, and of what the writers themselves as well as the Nobel Committee members have considered to be the primary qualities of good writing. If, after reading this book, the would-be laureate should relinquish his or her dream, then at least they may have gained some useful insights along the way.

It is now beginning to seem more and more likely, among scientists, philosophers and media commentators, that there are mysteries which are beyond the capacity of the human brain to unravel. One such unfathomable mystery is the manner in which the Swedish Academy selects a writer every year whom they have judged worthy of receiving the Nobel Prize in Literature. (Let it be noted straightaway that the preferred wording on the official website, nobelprize.org, is '*in*' and not '*for*' literature, though the latter might appear more logical to a native English speaker. It is clearly a direct translation of the Swedish 'Nobelpriset i litteratur'.)

It is possible to come very close to understanding the selection process but there always remains a core of uncertainty, which provides scope year after year for journalists, in particular, to speculate on the presence of political, moral and aesthetic bias in the Nobel Committee and in the Swedish Academy as a whole. Every year it seems that someone objects on some grounds or other. Doubtless sometimes the objections are valid, but when one attempts to trace a journalist's sources they almost inevitably turn out to be other journalists, who claims to have looked into the archives of the Swedish Academy, but precise quotable sources are rarely given. This core of uncertainty in one's knowledge regarding the selection process is generated by the policy of the Swedish Academy itself: no information about the Academy's deliberations is available for fifty years after any given award. This means that absolutely no one can access expert reports, correspondence and official minutes during that period. At present, the official website database provides information on the literature prize only for the period from the first award, in 1901, till 1950. Strictly speaking, and applying the fifty-year rule, information for the period 1951 to 1961 should now also be available on the database, but the Academy doesn't seem to have got its act together. I am informed by a secretary of the Academy that information for this period is available, but only in Swedish and only if I care to visit Stockholm. It is also clear that some of the more sensitive discussions over the years have been very much off the record. Of course there have been leaks: Academy members speaking carelessly over the akvavit and within the hearing of journalists. But the fifty-year rule has always made it difficult to openly confirm or deny.

Thus the verifiable and reliable sources for information on the Nobel Prize in Literature are few in number: the Nobel website and some publications by present and past members of the Academy and Nobel Committees.

It should also be remembered that the Swedish Academy is very much a closed shop: it has always eighteen members elected for life by existing members. New blood is introduced only when a chair becomes vacant. The actual Nobel Committee to advise on the award for literature consists of, at present, three to five of the current Academy members. There is also a board of experts in related fields whose help and advice they may call on, and an extensive reference library. The eighteen Academy members do not necessarily have to accept the committee's recommendations, and there have been many cases, as will be shown, where they have overruled them and made their own selection. It is a wonder therefore that the Nobel Prize in Literature has acquired such a revered status. Can such a self-perpetuating body really be the best forum for the assessment of the best literature of the day? However one answers this question, the Nobel Prizes are very much here to stay and many people throughout the world regard them as crowning achievements to aim for.

Readers should not come to this book with false expectations: it does not provide exhaustive summaries of the lives and works of all the literary laureates; some greatly respected writers are dealt with very cursorily, while several who have since fallen from grace are paid considerable attention. They are dealt with in accordance with the level of insight and advice they provide concerning the winning of the award and the nature of good writing. There are some writers who are scarcely mentioned at all, and this will doubtless lead to disappointment for some readers, but this omission should not be taken as a sign of disrespect for such writers' accomplishments. The style is occasionally flippant in tone with traces of irony and sarcasm: this is due to the fact that the author has considerable sympathy with the views of Jean-Paul Sartre, who, in his rejection of the prize, made it clear that he believed it impossible to rank writers. On the whole though, it is not such a bad thing to have prizes. Good writers very rarely get paid well, unless they are a dab hand at churning out best-sellers. The pen may be mightier than the sword, but it rarely wins honours and even more rarely brings back any spoils.

Some conventions in the text

There are frequent references to the three different kinds of speeches used at the Nobel Prize Ceremony. The Presentation Speech (sometimes referred to by the Nobel Organisation as Award Ceremony Speech) is one in which a member of the Academy introduces the laureate and his/her work. The Banquet Speech is a short speech given by the laureate on the occasion of the Nobel Banquet. The Nobel lecture is a talk, often of some length, on a topic of the laureate's choice. Banquet Speeches and Nobel Lectures are not always given, according to the laureate's circumstances and preferences.

A special convention has been used in the text to aid the reader. On the first occasion in a particular section when a laureate's name is mentioned, the date of the award is added in square brackets after the name. Also for the convenience of the reader a checklist of all the Nobel laureates in literature to date is provided at the end of the book, with basic information about the date of the award, country of origin/residence and language used. Space is left for the reader to keep the list up to date.

Origins and Ideals: The Rules of the Game

Being able to write well does not, by itself, guarantee consideration for the award of the Nobel Prize in Literature. While this
may appear at first surprising, it must be remembered that it is
simply assumed that all nominees have this ability. A writer who
is not vain enough to believe in the brilliance of his or her own
style must abandon all hope on entering the hellish realm of
competitive prize-winning. First be sure, therefore, that you can
write well: it is the *sine qua non* of everything else. Just as typists
should be able to spell, cyclists keep their balance and singers hit
the right notes. Having passed this first test of eligibility, there are
many more challenging conditions to fulfil, and eventual success
in winning the award depends on taking all of them into account.
To list just a few examples of such conditions, it depends very
much on what you write about; when, where and why you write;
how many of the right kind of people support you; the tastes and
preferences of the members of the Swedish Academy; which
other writers are nominated in the same year; how many compatriots have won it in the recent years; how many times you can
tolerate being nominated and rejected; whether you are actually
alive or can at least arrange to die at the right moment and, in all
probability, what the weather is like in Sweden on the day the
Nobel Committee meet to consider your nomination. Above all
that nebulous entity, the zeitgeist, has to be in just the right mood
to look favourably upon you.

It is worth therefore undertaking some study of the original criteria set up for the award and familiarising oneself with its general history. This will reveal just what the would-be laureate is up against. The quest is not a vain one, but the path to its acquisition is strewn with hazards, pitfalls and misunderstandings. Whoever expects to find a clear set of criteria for judgement and selection, which has been followed with consistency over the years, will be considerably disappointed.

If only Alfred Nobel had pondered over the wording of his will at greater length before committing the details to paper, he could have made the task of interpreting it that much easier for future generations.

What's in a Word? or Where There's a Will, There's Not Necessarily a Way

In his will, Alfred Nobel, after mature deliberation, and claiming in conclusion to have been of sound mind, declared that the realizable estate remaining after he had catered to the needs of various relatives, servants and other dependents, should be used to set up a unique fund, 'the interest on which shall be annually distributed in the form of prizes to those who, during the preceding year, shall have conferred the greatest benefit on mankind.'[1] Thus far the wording would appear to be reasonably unambiguous, though it already raises challenges and questions. It is necessary, for example, to ensure that one's literary masterpiece appears 'during the preceding year,' so that, on the assumption that one's nomination may not be successful on the first occasion, one must be prepared to produce at least one masterpiece per annum for an indefinite period. And how is one to be sure of having 'conferred the greatest benefit on mankind'? It would appear that it must be relatively easy to assess such benefit in the fields of natural science and in work carried out 'for fraternity between nations', that is for work deserving of the prize for peace. But to apply this criterion to works of literature begs so many questions about the nature and functions of literature. Nobel also stipulated that the interest on the fund should be divided into five equal parts, to be awarded as prizes, in five different areas of human endeavour. Literature is thus to be regarded as being on a par with the other four fields. It was in his description of the specific conditions for the award of the prize for literature that Nobel really set the cat among the pigeons. It all comes down to the interpretation of one particular Swedish word.

Here it is necessary to indulge in a brief linguistic diversion, delving into a few semantic and morphological mysteries of the Swedish language. Fortunately these mysteries have been clearly explained by a retired Swedish professor of computational linguistics, who has also been a Permanent Secretary of the Swedish Academy. In an essay published in 1997, entitled 'Topping Shakespeare? Aspects of the Nobel Prize for Literature', Professor Sture Allén explained that the word in Nobel's will which has caused all the problems is 'idealisk'. In the standard translation of the relevant clause in the will this is rendered as 'ideal'. Thus the prize in literature should be awarded 'to the person who shall have produced in the field of literature the most outstanding work in an ideal direction' ('den som inom litteraturen har producerat det utmärktaste i idealisk rigtning').[2] A close examination of the original handwritten will however reveals that Nobel had originally written a slightly different word, not 'idealisk', and then superimposed the 'sk' over the last part. Professor Allén has had the handwriting in the original will analysed under a microscope and has come to some intriguing conclusions. The first conclusion that can be drawn is that all the ink in that part of the text is of the same kind, suggesting that the alteration was probably made by Nobel at the time of writing. By enhancing the contrast and comparing the styles of different letters it was possible to conclude that Nobel had originally written 'idealirad'. It might appear that Nobel's alteration could be readily explained: the word 'idealirad' does not actually exist in the Swedish language, which Nobel was perfectly aware of, so he altered it to 'idealisk'. However the situation is complicated by the fact that there is another Swedish word which is very similar to Nobel's original non-existent word: 'idealiserad'. This is usually rendered in English as 'idealized'. Professor Allén provides a convincing interpretation of what may have happened, an explanation fully in accordance with Freud's theory of 'parapraxes' ('Freudian slips'). Allén suggests that Nobel was thinking of writing 'idealiserad', but was not satisfied that it was the right word to express what he meant. His doubt and hesitation caused him to misspell the word. Perhaps, suggests Allén, he 'wanted to use a word emphasizing loftiness without such an obvious reference to embellishment.'[3] That is to say that using the Swedish word for 'idealized' would imply something made more perfect, which Nobel did not want to stress. Thus, according to Allén's eyewitness account of the manuscript, Nobel superimposed the letters 'sk' over the final letters 'rad'.

While this interpretation clarifies the problem, narrowing the range of options somewhat, it still does not explain what Nobel meant by 'ideal direction'. There have been many attempts over the years to answer this question, but they have all been speculative and will doubtless continue to be so. Some are surprisingly extreme. Sture Allén tells us that the Danish literary critic Georg Brandes, who was living at about the same time as Nobel, reports in a letter that a close friend of Nobel told him that, as Nobel considered himself to be an anarchist, when he used the word which Brandes took to mean 'idealistic', he meant being critical of all social institutions, including marriage, the church and royalty. There are of course few actual laureates who would meet these criteria. The inventor of dynamite an anarchist? If true then it had the potential to become a lethal combination. Perhaps a member of the Swedish Academy, Artur Lundkvist, intended to forestall interpretation in that direction when he provided his own gloss: 'The prize should have an idealistic tendency; it should represent humanism. It cannot be awarded to those who advocate violence.'[4]

Probably one of the most famous interpretations of Nobel's intentions dates from the very beginning of the award and comes from the pen of one of Sweden's most internationally renowned writers, August Strindberg. He protested vehemently against the award in 1901 of the very first Nobel Prize in Literature to Sully Prudhomme. In his *Addresses to the Swedish Nation* of 1910, Strindberg wrote: '…the prizewinner should have written *ideally* (later tampered with to make it *idealistically*, which is something else), but he was a materialist and had translated Lucretius.'[5] There was thus a clear distinction, in Strindberg's mind at least, between 'ideal' and 'idealistic' (and their adverbial forms). After analyzing further the cognates of 'ideal', not only in Strindberg's works but in those of other contemporary writers, Allén comes to the conclusion that for Nobel 'idealisk' did not mean 'having the quality of the ideal', but 'referring to an ideal'. But this does nothing to rid Nobel's words of their vagueness and ambiguity. There is still some justification therefore in criticizing him for indulging in the ill-formulated ramblings of an elderly man in what is a crucial legal document. On the other hand he might be praised for his supreme almost unearthly wisdom. By stipulating that his prize should go to the author of 'an outstanding work in an ideal direction', he was making it possible for each succeeding generation to define the terms of the will according to its own priorities of taste, morality and ideals of humanity.

There are also other more general guidelines in the will however, which have aided the Academy in its interpretation of the will and in drawing up its shortlist of candidates. Two of these three general guidelines relate more to matters of formal eligibility: the work should have been produced 'during the previous year', and there shall be no consideration of the nationality of the candidate. The third is a crucial stipulation for all the Nobel Prizes: the prizes shall be awarded 'to those who… shall have conferred the greatest benefit on mankind.'[6] It would seem therefore that this must be an essential component of the ideal striven for.

Death and Deconstruction

Alfred Nobel determined that there should be no doubt whatsoever about his eventual demise (10th December 1896). He wanted to be sure of being well and truly dead: 'Finally, it is my express wish that following my death my veins shall be opened, and when this has been done and competent Doctors have confirmed clear signs of death, my remains shall be cremated in a so-called crematorium.'[7] Perhaps he feared that if his spirit continued to haunt a body reduced to a vegetative state with all the appearances of death, he would be driven to distraction at having to witness the ways in which others were interpreting his last will and testament.

He would have had to vegetate for quite some time however before perceiving that his wishes had been realised. First the Nobel Foundation had to be set up and finally, in June 1900, its statutes ratified. The Nobel Foundation was established as a private institution to manage the finances and administer the Nobel Prize awards. Only when its statutes had been ratified could the Swedish Academy set to work on preparing to award the first Nobel Prizes. In another example of his vagueness, Nobel had specified in the will only that the prize for literature should be awarded 'by the Academy in Stockholm'.[8] The Nobel Foundation decided that he obviously meant by this the Swedish Academy.

The Foundation also took it upon themselves to define more precisely what they considered to be implied by Nobel's use of the word 'literature': 'not only belles-lettres, but also other writings, which, by virtue of their form and style, possess literary value'.[9] This enabled them of course to award the prize to virtually anyone whom they deemed worthy of it. Literature was thus, tautologically, that which had 'literary value'.

The time restriction was also essentially nullified, by specifying that works presented 'during the preceding year' could be interpreted to include also older works, the greatness of which had only just been recognized. They could be considered 'if their significance has not become apparent until recently'.[10] In practice and in fairness to the Academy, the selection committee has always endeavoured to stay as close to the spirit of the will as possible if not to the letter of it. They have not wanted to appear to be inflexible. But Dante, Shakespeare, Goethe and Dickens were indubitably too long dead.

The Nobel Foundation also formulated rules, which have been modified over the years, in its statutes, defining who was eligible to nominate candidates, and what the procedure of selection should be. To be sure of producing works that can win over nominators and eventually the judges however, the would-be laureate needs first and foremost to know what kinds of writing have earned consideration for the prize over the years, what endowed them with that nebulous quality of 'literary value', and what aspects of the contemporary world have affected the selection criteria. Only then will it be possible to hazard a guess at what criteria might prevail at the present time. Over the first hundred years or so of the awards, Nobel's words have been deconstructed again and again, to make them applicable to issues and concerns of the day. A brief history of the changes in the interpretation of what constitutes the ideal in literature reads like a genealogy of the values of modern literary taste.

The Origin of Speciousness, or The Evolution of Literary Taste by the Process of Unnatural Selection

There is a major hindrance to discovering what considerations the Academy have actually taken into account when coming to their final selection of prizewinners: the fifty-year ban on access to all information relating to the awards. Thus, at the time of writing, there is very little information available on the awards made after 1961 (and, as you will recall, the database on the official website only goes up to 1950). One can make some reasonable assumptions about criteria adhered to in recent years however based on various public pronouncements by members of the Academy and especially by studying the Presentation Speeches made in each case. In some cases the Banquet Speeches, perhaps under the influence of good wines and probably a few good champagnes, yield revealing insights. For the period prior to 1951 more detailed information is available on the official website. While it is difficult to come to any firm conclusions on the extent to which the interests and prejudices of the individual members of the Nobel Committee (usually only three to five Academy members) may have influenced the selection, it does seem that, in the early years at least, the preferences expressed by the committee reflected very closely the tastes of its chairpersons. This has become less noticeable as the years have passed. The chairperson has, incidentally, sometimes also been the Permanent Secretary of the Academy, but not always at the same time. Though it is not possible to draw clear distinctions between periods, certain traits have emerged. The following temporal divisions are therefore approximate.

Scaling the Moral High Ground (1901–12 approx.)

The laureates chosen under the chairmanship of Carl David af Wirsén (from the beginnings until April 1912) clearly reflect his preferences and ideology. Wirsén had a distinguished career before he became a member of the Academy. He had specialized in French literature and also taught and published on Swedish literature. From 1876 he had been both librarian and art curator in Gothenburg. He was a recognised poet and writer of hymns, wrote literary reviews, and collaborated on the Academy's dictionary. He was thus well on the way to becoming a possible candidate for the Nobel Prize himself. He held strong conservative views, believing in the need to uphold the values of the state and the church as pillars of society, and supporting traditional family values. It is not surprising therefore to find him decrying the works of his fellow countryman August Strindberg, as well as Henrik Ibsen, Émile Zola and Leo Tolstoy.

In his Presentation Speech for the very first Nobel Prize in Literature Wirsén revealed clearly the extent to which his own philosophy had influenced the choice of the French philosopher and poet Sully Prudhomme. After much talk of Prudhomme's 'cosmopolitan aspirations' and the fact that he was 'an advocate of peace and the brotherhood of nations', Wirsén described the main themes of his work as 'love of the spiritual, his doubts, his sorrows, which nothing earthly can dissipate'. The presence of high moral idealism is most clearly emphasized towards the end of Wirsén's speech. For him Prudhomme found 'evidence of man's supernatural destiny in the moral realm, in the voice of conscience, and in the lofty and undeniable prescriptions of duty'. He represented 'better than most writers what the testator called "an idealistic tendency" in literature'.[11]

And there we have yet another rendering of Nobel's 'idealisk riktning'.

Perceptive modern readers might find themselves wondering whether Prudhomme's high moral idealism is one of the reasons why it is difficult to find editions of his works nowadays let alone readers of them.

The award of the prize to the historian, Theodor Mommsen, in 1902, was justified by reference to the Nobel statutes which sanction the choice of 'also other writings that in form or content show literary value'. Mommsen was also a giant among historians of his time and a polymath (amongst other fields he was also an expert in Roman Law, epigraphy and numismatics). In his Presentation Speech Wirsén again revealed his sympathies for the laureate's ideals. He praised Mommsen's depiction of 'how the Roman's obedience to the state was linked to the obedience of son to father', and clearly felt close to Mommsen in the historian's belief 'that every state is built on sand unless the ruler and the government are tied together by a common morality. A healthy family life is to him the core of the nation.'[12]

With the weakening of the concept of the nuclear family and the evaporation of a shared morality, it is not surprising that few modern readers feel drawn to Mommsen's writings, except for Germans and specialist historians (and among them mainly German specialist historians).

Wirsén made most of the Presentation Speeches during his tenancy of the chair but not all of them (the exceptions were in 1908, 1909 and 1912). He praised the Norwegian Bjørnstjerne Bjørnson in 1903 for his 'purest and most elevated ideas' and for how his genius put 'the highest demands on human life'. Though many may have thought these ideals too high, '...in their noble severity they are infinitely preferable to the laxness that is all too prevalent in the literature of our day'.[13] Wirsen's evaluations of the qualities of the other laureates during this period are consistent throughout with this high moral idealism.

Neutral but Nice (1913–21 approx.)

Under Harald Hjärne's chairmanship the selection policy of the Academy underwent several significant changes. Whether this was due to his own ideals and influence or to the majority of opinions on the Nobel Committee it is difficult to determine. Some of the modifications were deemed necessary in response to changes in the world at large.

Hjärne was certainly a more liberally minded man than Wirsén, though he retained a strong nationalist commitment. He had been trained as a historian, held several professorships at leading Swedish universities, and was a member of a number of learned societies. He was also actively involved in various political issues of the day, such as voting rights, and matters concerning unions and national defence. For some time he was a parliamentary representative. It is likely that his antipathy to the conflicts between the great European powers on the eve of the First World War and during it contributed to the notable bias in favour of authors from Scandinavian and neutral countries in this period. Apart from one award to the first non-European (Rabindranath Tagore in 1913) and two awards to French writers (Romain Rolland in 1915 and Anatole France in 1921), one of the others went to Sweden itself (Verner von Heidenstam in 1916), one to Norway (Knut Hamsun in 1920), and two to Denmark (Karl Adolph Gjellerup and Henrik Pontoppidan in 1917, one of only four occasions when the award has been made to two writers at the same time). Possibly the most neutral of all countries, Switzerland, received its first Nobel Prize in literature in 1919, when it was awarded to Carl Spitteler. It is also noteworthy that the first two occasions when the prize was *not* awarded occurred in this period too, notably 1914 and 1918, at the outbreak and then the end of the First World War.

Stylish but Universal (1922–43 approx.)

When Hjärne died in 1922, Per Hallström took over to become one of the longest serving chairmen (until 1946). Under his guidance good style and universal relevance became central concerns in the selection of laureates. This also meant that many innovative and experimental writers were not considered.

Hallström is himself well-known as a poet, dramatist and short story writer, and was also proposed as a candidate for the prize. His writing is very much admired for the depth of its compassion and its sensitivity to beauty. Under his chairmanship the stipulation 'in an ideal direction' was even more freely interpreted, though always with the general requisite for all Nobel Prizewinners: that their works confer 'the greatest benefit on mankind'. This paved the way for the re-nomination of George

Bernard Shaw in 1925, who had been rejected earlier. Something of Hallström's own aesthetic sensitivity is perhaps reflected in the selection of William Butler Yeats in 1923, Thomas Mann in 1929 and John Galsworthy in 1932.

In the 1930s the criterion of 'universal interest', was stressed by the committee, which they interpreted as implying writers whose works were accessible to all. Thus obscure or exclusive writers stood little chance of selection. For these reasons Paul Valéry and Paul Claudel were declined in favour of more popular writers such as Sinclair Lewis in 1930 and Pearl S. Buck in 1938.

For the four years of 1940 to 1943, when Europe was at war yet again, the prize was not awarded.

Innovative and Profound (1940–60s approx.)

After a long period in which no Nobel Prize in Literature was awarded, the Nobel Committee finally got its act together again in 1944 and reviewed the criteria required by Nobel's will yet again. Hallström was still chairman until 1946 when he was succeeded by Anders Österling, who held the post until 1970. Perhaps the war had shaken up the committee's sensitivities somewhat, for it now decided that popularity and accessibility were not lofty enough qualities to be sought if the Nobel Prize was to retain its respected status.

Perhaps the war had also disturbed the conscience and spirits of the members of the committee and enabled them to contemplate the possibility of considering more disturbing, more profound and even pessimistic writers. Was it not after all for the good of all mankind to have its conscience thoroughly rattled from time to time? Perhaps literary laurels should be awarded, as in the sciences, to those writers who had made new developments and opened up new possibilities in literature, who had provided a new way of looking at the world and displayed fresh, innovative use of language? Thus the committee found itself able to choose Hermann Hesse in 1946, whom it had rejected earlier for his 'ethical anarchy' amongst other negative aspects of his writing. Hesse was followed by André Gide in 1947, T.S. Eliot in 1948, and William Faulkner in 1949. Other outstanding innovators chosen were Albert Camus in 1957 and the French poet Saint-John Perse in 1960. Perhaps an especially free interpretation of Nobel's criteria came with the selection of Samuel Beckett in 1969. In his Presentation Speech, Karl Ragnar Gierow, at the time the Permanent Secretary of the Academy but who would become the next chairman of the committee in the following year, explained that the committee had discovered a profound humanism in Beckett's bleak vision of the world.

Celebrating Difference (From the late 60s onwards)

One noticeable phenomenon from the late 1960s onwards is the widening of the 'catchment area'. The committee started to consider more readily the works of writers who had not only been innovative but who had also encouraged and raised the standards of literature in their countries, many now well outside the boundaries of Europe. The depiction of the lives of Jewish people living in Israel by Shmuel Yosef Agnon was honoured in 1966; the evocation of the lives of the Indian peoples of Latin America won the award for Miguel Ángel Asturias in 1967; Yasunari Kawabata's insight into Japanese life won him the prize in 1968; and there followed prizes for Pablo Neruda (Chile, 1971), Patrick White (Australia, 1973), Gabriel García Márquez (Columbia, 1982), Wole Soyinka (Nigeria, 1986) and Naguib Mahfouz (Egypt, 1988). The trend has continued to the present day.

Also from the late 1970s onwards, many academicians felt it was time they honoured outstanding writers who had not yet gained universal recognition, giving them, in other words, the attention they deserved. In this category can be considered the awards to Isaac Bashevis Singer (USA, 1978), Odysseus Elytis (Greece, 1979),

Elias Canetti (UK, 1981) and Jaroslav Seifert (Czechoslovakia, 1984). This criterion has continued to be regarded as important up to the present, with special focus on poets who would otherwise not have gained a worldwide audience, such as Octavio Paz (Mexico, 1990), Derek Walcott (Saint Lucia, 1992), Seamus Heaney (Ireland, 1995) and Wisława Szymborska (Poland, 1996).

But there is still scope for consideration of writers long recognised for their greatness but who have been overlooked for prizes in the past: for example Günter Grass (Germany, 1999), J.M. Coetzee (South Africa, 2003), Harold Pinter (UK, 2005) and Doris Lessing (UK, 2007).

Horses for Courses or The Literary Steeplechase

Having identified as far as possible the nature of the zeitgeist (what kind of writers the Nobel Committee might be looking out for at any given time), the next condition the would-be laureate must fulfil is: over-all fitness and stamina to survive the complex obstacle course ahead. Much will depend on the support that can be mustered from compatriots, and from a few internationally renowned literary critics thrown in for good measure. No mean challenge.

The procedure is clearly and unequivocally laid down by the Swedish Academy. The preliminary conditions are stated in paragraphs 7 and 8 of the Statutes of the Nobel Foundation[14]. Firstly, personal application is completely out of the question. One must be 'nominated in writing by a person competent to make such a nomination' (§7). This of course immediately begs the question how one identifies someone with such competency. Then after having identified such a person or persons (by a specific glance perhaps, or a Masonic-style handshake?), one must be sure to keep a careful eye on the calendar and make sure that the competent person is in full possession of all the necessary paperwork, for nominations must be 'submitted during the preceding twelve months up to February 1' (§7) and 'be explained and accompanied by the publications and other documents cited in support of them'(§8).

All questions and doubts are resolved by the detailed guidelines provided by the Swedish Academy on its own website. Those persons competent to make nominations are:

1. Members of the Swedish Academy and of other academies, institutions and Societies which are similar to it in construction and purpose;
2. Professors of literature and of linguistics at universities and university colleges;
3. Previous Nobel Laureates in Literature;
4. Presidents of those societies of authors that are representatives of the literary production in their respective countries.[15]

All this makes it abundantly clear that one must not only be a brilliant writer in tune with the zeitgeist, but one must also cultivate a large circle of sympathetic and influential friends in the right academic and literary circles: it would be advantageous therefore to join as many prestigious associations as possible, including among them writers' unions and the like, hobnob with relevant professors at conferences, attend writers' festivals and ingratiate yourself with renowned authors, and endeavour to start up a correspondence with former literary laureates.

If you have found at least a handful of competent and willing nominators, then the initial hurdles have been overcome. Having ensured that you can trust in their commitment, you must then put yourself completely in their hands. They must put the nomination forward to the Nobel Committee, using all the necessary documentation you will have supplied. Thereafter there is nothing that the nominee can do, while the committee does its preparatory work. Lobbying, in any form, is completely out of the question.

The Nobel Year (1st February – 10th December)

The first task facing the Nobel Committee, when a nomination arrives (the deadline is currently 31st January), is to check that it has come from one of the authorized sources. Invented institutes and fictional professors will soon be discovered. If the source is clearly unauthorized, the application will simply be ignored. The committee then presents its list of approved nominations to the Academy early in February. As soon as the list has been ratified by the Academy it is returned to the Nobel Committee.

Even if authorized, many of the names will be eliminated at an early stage for various reasons: lack of good literary style and quality, or because their works are not essentially literary in nature or contain objectionable ideological or nationalistic ideas, etc.

The applications remaining are then studied in more detail. At this stage further expert assessment can be sought, and if the works are in a minority language, special translations can be commissioned.

In April the committee puts the results of its research to the Academy in the form of a preliminary list of about fifteen to twenty candidates. When the Academy has approved this preliminary list, it is sent back again to the committee, and by the end of May the committee supplies the definitive list of priority candidates. This list usually consists of only five names, and the Academy has the right to add or remove names.

The Academy members then spend the summer holidays reading any of the works by the five shortlisted authors with which they are unfamiliar. Each Nobel Committee member also has to prepare an individual report to be delivered to the Academy at the first meeting in the autumn, in mid-September. The choice of the winner must be made by early or mid-October. To win, a candidate must receive more than half the votes cast. The prizewinner then receives the prize, which consists of a medal and a sum of money (the latest figure on the official website is about ten million kronor for 2009) from the King of Sweden in Stockholm Concert Hall on 10th December (Nobel Day).

Modifications have been made to the procedure over the years. Nowadays, for example, the Nobel Committee sends out actual invitations, in September of the year prior to the year of the award, to between 600 and 700 individuals and organisations which are qualified to nominate.

Under Starter's Orders

If you feel that you have been able in your writing to identify the zeitgeist correctly, are confident of gaining the trust and admiration of powerful and influential persons competent to nominate, and can otherwise fulfil the requirements of the statutes of the Nobel Foundation, then you may still not be quite ready to face the gruelling race ahead. Many favourites have fallen and never gained the prize. It would be wise to study in depth the cautionary accounts of the successes and failures, the triumphs and pitfalls, of the great and the not so great, as described in the following pages.

Famous Refusals

Before proceeding a single step further it would be wise to square the pursuit of literary glory with your conscience. So far it has been assumed that the will and drive to win the award was self-evident. Why else, your eye having been caught by this book's title, would you already be plunging into the second chapter? But, to echo the equestrian metaphors of the first chapter, before you gallop boldly over the many fences before you, it would be wise to be sure of your ground, your moral ground that is, be it high or low. If it be low (fame, medal, money), at least be honest about it, but if it be high (recognition as a model both for other writers and for the rest of humanity), then be sure that your ground is really firm. Can you honestly say that you deserve it? And remember that if you are so presumptuous and wish to assert confidently that you know of no one more deserving, then remember that this implies recognition of the validity of the whole process of awarding Nobel Prizes. After all if you wish to be canonized you have to accept the doctrines of your church. And you should be ready to defend your worthiness at all times. Thus to proceed with confidence and determination you should make yourself familiar with the arguments of the Devil's Advocate, and be able to counter them. The Devil's Advocate in the history of the Nobel Prize in Literature was Jean-Paul Sartre.

More Equal than Others? or The Reluctant Swine

In 1964 the following announcement was made by Anders Österling, the chairman of the Nobel Committee:

> This year the Nobel Prize in Literature has been granted by
> the Swedish Academy to the French writer Jean-Paul Sartre
> for his work which, rich in ideas and filled with the spirit
> of freedom and the quest for truth, has exerted a far-reach-
> ing influence on our age.[16]

There is nothing a writer could object to in such an appreciation
of his or her endeavours and the Academy's choice is clearly
in keeping with its concern in the post-war period to show pref-
erence for writers who were innovative and profound. But then
Österling reminded his audience:

> It will be recalled that the laureate has made it known that
> he did not wish to accept the prize. The fact that he has
> declined this distinction does not in the least modify the
> validity of the award. Under the circumstances, however, the
> Academy can only state that the presentation of the prize
> cannot take place.[17]

The Academy had therefore found itself in a dilemma. According
to Clause 10 of their statutes, the Academy is not allowed to with-
draw the award once it had been announced, so like all good
committees they decided on a compromise, and like many a compromise it involved quibbling with words: the prize would be
awarded but not awarded. It would be announced and recorded in
the archives but not actually given. There was no way they could
change their mind and choose someone else, because that would
be to undermine the validity of the whole selection process.

One question must have occurred to many outside the secret
enclave of the Academy: had no one in the previous sixty-three

years of the history of the Nobel Prizes considered asking nominees if they were happy to be nominated? It could have avoided a lot of agonizing and controversy. Presumably the Academy had always assumed the unshakeable vanity of all mankind: who could possibly refuse to be honoured by such an illustrious body as theirs? Thus having made their decision and worked out their justification for it (after many a sleepless night no doubt), the committee stuck to it.

It should be pointed out here that Sartre was not the first to refuse. The other notorious case was that of Boris Pasternak in 1958. The formulation of the statement about the impossibility of rescinding the award in Sartre's case does clearly reveal that Österling had checked the wording of his speech in 1958.

At the banquet for the awards in 1964, S. Friberg, Rector of the Caroline Institute, made a speech justifying the committee's decision concerning Sartre. He openly admitted that the Nobel awards always attract controversy, and there is more than a hint of reprimand that the general public does not really understand such things and should leave such judgments to the experts:

> There is always discussion about this prize, which every one considers himself capable of judging, or which he does not understand and consequently criticizes.[18]

He went on to praise the qualities of Sartre's work which enabled it to satisfy the conditions stipulated by Nobel. His work had been 'sustained by a profoundly serious endeavour to improve the reader, the world at large'.[19] In conclusion Friberg praised Sartre however for the very aspects of his thought which led him, on his own admission, to refuse to accept the prize. For Sartre standardization and placement in hierarchical structures (by awarding prizes which recognized achievements of specific values) meant the loss of individual freedom. Friberg perceived this but failed to realize the irony of the situation:

The quality of human life depends not only on external conditions but also on individual happiness. In our age of standardization and complex social systems, awareness of the meaning of life for the individual has perhaps not been lost, but it has certainly been dulled; and it is as urgent for us today as it was in Nobel's time to uphold the ideals which were his.[20]

Sartre first made public his views concerning the prize in an article in *Le Figaro* of 23rd October 1964. He revealed in this that he had sent a letter to the Academy expressing the wish that the award should not be made to him. In his official announcement of the refusal Anders Österling reported Sartre's assertion that in refusing he had no intention of slighting the Academy. He had made the decision for 'personal and objective reasons'[21] of his own. These 'personal and objective reasons' should be the special concern of our would-be laureate.

By personal reasons Sartre meant that to accept such an honour would be 'to associate his personal commitments with the awarding institution' (Österling). His acceptance would mean allowing himself to be turned into an institution. He would become 'The Nobel Prize Writer', a figure in the state hierarchy, and indeed in that of the world. For similar reasons he had declined to accept membership of the Légion d'honneur and refused to enter the Collège de France. He was thus consistent in his objections.

By objective reasons it seems that Sartre meant to imply criticism of the very notion of a prize-giving institution. For him cultural interchange should take place between men, between whole cultures, and even more broadly between East and West, without the mediation of institutions. Reviewing the history of the Nobel Prize awards in the past he did not feel that they had represented equally writers of all nations and all ideologies. It is a view that we shall find echoed on other occasions.

Thus if the would-be laureate is beginning to feel sympathy with at least some of Sartre's views, then it is time to take stock of his, or her, conscience. Are they willing to become a pillar of the state, functioning, albeit unwittingly, as a pawn in a game of international cultural diplomacy? Would they be putting their individuality and freedom as a writer at risk?

In conversations which took place during the summer of 1974 and were recorded and written down by Simone de Beauvoir, Sartre's decision to reject the Nobel Prize can be understood in the broader context of his ideas and moral principles. He confirmed that he had always, since his schooldays, opposed all attempts to classify human beings in hierarchies. He was convinced that what he felt to be true of himself should be the right of all human beings: 'My being was that deep subjective reality which was beyond everything that could be said about it and which could not be classified.'[22] The grading of human beings was of course unavoidable to some degree, especially in relation to their job functions, and Sartre recognized this. Hierarchies were primarily concerned with grading jobs in this way. But people who allowed themselves to be limited to their positions in such hierarchies could not achieve their potential and remained less than human. Sartre did not hesitate to label such people swine: 'The swine are people who commit their freedom to being acknowledged as good by others...'[23] By this definition are not all those who knowingly allow their nominations for the Nobel Prize in Literature to go forward essentially porcine in nature?

De Beauvoir then asked him whether it was his feeling for the equality between all men that had led him to reject all formal honours. His reply was much more forceful than those polite words he had written in his letter to the Academy and in his public announcement in *Le Figaro*. He was dismissive of any group of people who set themselves up to pass value judgements on others. His words are unequivocal:

These honours are given by men to other men, and the men who give the honour, whether it's the *Légion d'honneur* or the Nobel Prize, are not qualified to give it. I can't see who has the right to give Kant or Descartes or Goethe a prize which means *Now you belong in a classification. We have turned literature into a graduated reality and in that literature you occupy such and such a rank*. I reject the possibility of doing that, and therefore I reject all honours.[24]

But as most people are submitted to hierarchical systems they come to prefer being in a hierarchy to accepting the freedom of their own fundamental being, perhaps because the latter is too challenging. It is far easier to let someone else make decisions and value judgements. In this way honours are rated too highly. For Sartre however they correspond to nothing: 'They correspond only to a distinction given in a hierarchy of being that is not real...'[25]

De Beauvoir then discussed with him some prizes which he had nevertheless accepted. His defence is reasonable. The Populist Prize he had accepted in 1940, even though he felt he had little in common with the Populist movement, quite simply because it was wartime, which he felt devalued all prizes, and in such desperate times he needed the money. Another prize, which Sartre referred to as 'The Italian Prize', he accepted because it was awarded by the Italian communists for his intellectual resistance during the German occupation of France, and he felt it had nothing to do with hierarchies and honours. Then de Beauvoir brought him back to discussion of the Nobel Prize, 'the most notorious of your refusals'. He replied with perhaps his most critical attack on the whole notion of literary awards. It is worth quoting it in full:

What does it mean, saying that a writer had it in 1974, what does it mean in relation to the men who had it earlier or to those who have not had it but who also write and are perhaps better? What does the prize mean? Can it really be said that the year they gave it to me I was superior to my colleagues, the other writers, and that the year after it was someone else who was superior?[26]

He continued to emphasize what he considered to be the absurdities of such an institution: if a writer had in fact been superior to others for some years, why should he be singled out as superior in any one year? If he is the best, or the equal of all the best writers, is he not their equal forever? He had noticed that in order to be awarded the prize a writer had to provide evidence of having made 'a little fresh spurt', as though in proof that he was still mentally alert. In his case he felt that it had probably been the recent publication of his autobiographical reflections under the title *Words* which had made the Academy feel that he was still creatively alive. But this meant that the year before, when he had not had a fresh work published, he was in their eyes worth less. He then returned to his primary objection to such prizes on the grounds that they fix writers into hierarchies:

The whole idea of arranging literature in a hierarchical order is one that is completely contrary to the literary idea. On the other hand it is perfectly suitable for a bourgeois society that wants to make everything an integral part of a system.[27]

He then took the example of Hemingway (awarded the prize in 1954). He had known Hemingway personally, was fond of him and had visited him in Cuba. 'But the idea of being his equal or of holding any rank at all in relation to him was very far from my mind. There is an idea here that I think naïve and even stupid.'[28]

The Prince and the Rabble

Sartre should not be allowed to dazzle us too much however with all his talk of equality. In the same conversations with de Beauvoir he talked of his younger days. He had obviously had no problem reconciling the notion of the equality of all men with the sense of his own superiority. The genius for him was the person who became aware of their full potential as a human being, so that he clearly visualized a two-tier hierarchy at least consisting of those beings who remained 'raw material' and those who were able to realize themselves. When he was a schoolboy he already had an inkling of this distinction, and of the inherent paradox. His grandfather had regarded him as a little prince, which implied an essential superiority:

> If a being possesses this subjective reality of princehood it does not lead to equality, for a prince is superior to those around him. Yet there is a kind of equality at the bottom of all this, because I believed that I was a human being and that all human beings were therefore princes...So there was one kind of world made up of equals, who were princes, and then the rabble.[29]

Writer's Bloc

The other famous case of refusal to accept the Nobel Prize in Literature is that of Boris Pasternak in 1958. But the circumstances were completely different to those of Sartre: he did not refuse on principle. It can be argued that he really had no option. It is a story that verges on tragedy, and the lesson it teaches the would-be laureate is clear and stark: do not allow your name to be put forward if you are living under a totalitarian regime that does not take kindly to notions of free speech, negative criticism and broadly humanistic ideals.

The bald announcement by Anders Österling of the award to Pasternak reveals nothing of the furore it was to cause. The award was made to him 'for his notable achievement in both contemporary poetry and the field of the great Russian narrative tradition'. Österling reminded his audience that Pasternak had declined the distinction and added, in the same words he was to use in Sartre's case, that 'This refusal, of course, in no way alters the validity of the award.' And he regretted 'that the presentation of the prize cannot take place'.[30]

Pasternak had sent two telegrams to the Swedish Academy, the first in modest acknowledgment and the second in rejection of the honour. On 25th October 1958 he wrote 'Immensely thankful, touched, proud, astonished, abashed.' Then four days later on the 29th he wrote 'Considering the meaning this reward has been given in the society to which I belong, I must reject this undeserved prize which has been presented to me. Please do not receive my voluntary rejection with displeasure.'[31] He had obviously chosen his words very carefully, so as not to offend the Soviet government, which is not mentioned by name. He mentioned that the rejection was 'voluntary', which is to say that it was not forced on him. The opposite was in fact the case. The background to his decision is complex and steeped in political intrigue and emotional blackmail.

It is important to bear in mind the political situation in the Soviet Union at the time. Stalin had died in 1953 and by the mid-1950s Nikita Khrushchev had established his power base. In 1956 he denounced Stalin's use of repression and started to ease controls over both party and society in general. But the freedoms in the Eastern Bloc were relative and Communist party doctrine still remained sacrosanct. It was also in 1956 that the Soviet Union used military force against anti-communist uprisings in Poland and Hungary.

Pasternak had reason indeed to be wary and anxious: he had endured many years of insecurity as a writer. He had made no attempt to flee abroad after the Bolsheviks seized power in

October 1917 but he retained serious doubts about the methods employed by the government. He continued to write and translate but found it impossible to get works published in book form. Like many others at that time he declaimed his works in 'literary cafés' or circulated them in manuscript form. His volume of poetry, *My Sister, Life*, was not published until 1921. Under the dictatorship of Joseph Stalin he had to modify his style greatly to get anything published at all. Reluctant to conform to the aesthetic principles of Socialist Realism, he turned for some time to translating works of foreign masters, such as Goethe, Shakespeare and Rilke. In 1934 a close friend and fellow writer, Osip Mandelstam, was arrested for his epigram attacking Stalin, and Pasternak was contacted directly from the Kremlin by telephone: Stalin asked him for his opinion of Mandelstam. His own freedom was directly threatened in 1937 when he refused to sign a statement organized by the Union of Soviet Writers supporting the death penalty for two military figures in a show trial. When Stalin died in 1953, there were no immediate signs of thaw or amnesty, and the woman with whom Pasternak conducted a long-lasting extra-marital relationship, Olga Ivinskaya, was imprisoned in a gulag. Pasternak was convinced that this was an attempt by the secret police to extract evidence from her which could be used in a trial against him. In 1956 he finished the novel he had started work on much earlier, *Doctor Zhivago*. It was rejected by the literary magazine *Novy Mir* which condemned its implied criticism of Socialist Realism. The censors also found evidence of anti-communist sympathies. It was this work of course which was to make him world-famous and finally swing the Nobel Committee in his favour. The story of *Doctor Zhivago*'s eventual publication and submission to the committee however is the stuff of an espionage thriller.

Pasternak and Olga arranged for the British scholar and writer Sir Isaiah Berlin to smuggle the manuscript of the novel abroad, and in 1957 the billionaire Italian publisher Giangiacomo Feltrinelli published the first edition of it in Italian. *Il Dottor Zivago* became an immediate success, due partly to the Soviet campaign against it. The Soviet authorities demanded that it be withdrawn, but Feltrinelli refused to alter his publication plans, which resulted in his expulsion from the Italian Communist party. The first English translation of the work by Max Hayward and Manya Harari was available by August 1958. Over the period from 1958 to 1959 it was at the top of *The New York Times* bestseller list for twenty-six weeks. There was an inevitable backlash in the Soviet Union. The Union of Soviet Writers expelled Pasternak and sent a petition to the Politburo demanding that he be stripped of his Soviet citizenship and exiled to the West.

In January 2007, Peter Finn of the *Washington Post* foreign service reported on a forthcoming book, *The Laundered Novel* by Ivan Tolstoy, which made extraordinary claims that the CIA were involved in the publication of a Russian edition of Pasternak's novel. Tolstoy is a writer and broadcaster for Radio Free Europe and Radio Liberty in Munich, and in an article published on the organization website (20th February 2009) he explained the motivation for the pirate edition as he perceived it: 'Although the Swedish Academy is famously protective of its rules for eligibility, it has long been believed an author must be published in his native language in order to be considered for the prize.'[32] The claim was therefore that this limited edition helped Pasternak win the Nobel Prize. Tolstoy's book was to stir up a hornet's nest of argument and counter-argument in the usual way of conspiracy theories. Finn reports that Tolstoy had said to him in a telephone conversation: 'Pasternak's novel became a tool that was used by the United States to teach the Soviet Union a lesson.'[33] There is no scope in the context of the present work to provide an extensive account clarifying the murky blend of theory and conjecture, fact and fiction with which the whole affair has been clouded. As a story of cold-war intrigue it is compelling reading, but its thesis that the CIA indirectly (or directly) influenced the decision of the Swedish Academy is seriously flawed. In the article published on the RFE / RL website Tolstoy further claimed that he had 'spent nearly 20 years travelling the world in search of more clues.'[34] It is an assumption common among many non-academic researchers that the amount of time spent on research somehow strengthens one's arguments.

What Tolstoy believes happened can be summarized briefly. A pirated edition of the Russian text of *Doctor Zhivago* was undoubtedly published in The Hague in September 1958. It was believed that this was based on a photocopy of a Russian copy in the possession of Giangiacomo Feltrinelli. The novel had been published by Feltrinelli in Italian in 1957. Feltrinelli himself explained in an interview with *The Sunday Times* his version of what happened: 'I commissioned a limited edition of *Doctor Zhivago* in Russian from a printing shop in Holland but to my deep surprise a different, pirated Russian edition appeared in Holland...'[35] Feltrinelli's son Carlo, in his book about his father, speculated about CIA involvement and mentions allegations that a copy of the book was obtained by cloak-and-dagger means: 'Let us note in parentheses that the CIA seemed to be partly involved in that affair. I mean the attempts at a pirate edition of the book. I read somewhere that Her Majesty's Intelligence Service did not leave this book without its attention. Allegedly, they photographed the typescript at the Malta airport when the plane Feltrinelli was traveling in made a bogus emergency landing.'[36] A senior Russian academic, Anna Sergeyeva-Klyatis, has argued that Carlo's account was very much dependent on a speculative article reprinted from the German magazine *Der Spiegel* in a pro-Soviet Berlin newspaper (the title of which translates as 'For Return to Homeland'). These are the sources for the main plot of Tolstoy's book. The incident in Malta is described by Sergeyeva-Klyatis as being 'adorned with stunning fictional details'.[37] She quotes from Tolstoy's book:

Suddenly for no apparent reason the plane landed in Malta. The propellers went still. It was getting dark. A herd of gesticulating passengers was unhurriedly streaming towards the lights of the one-storey airport building. All plans for the evening had gone to pot. But in the autumn twilight that day in 1956 there were several gentlemen in the Malta airport whose plans for the evening were completely contrary to the needs of the passengers: they needed the plane to change its course and land precisely in that airport. After the passengers had been seated in the waiting room a certain suitcase was found in the plane's belly and a plump folder containing a typescript was removed from it. It took two hours to secretly photocopy the 600-page manuscript in the airport office under the light of specially brought lamps; it was then put back into the suitcase upon which the passengers returned to the airplane. The propellers resumed their droning as if nothing had happened. And thus the typescript of *Doctor Zhivago* got into the hands of Western intelligence services.[38]

Under the Swedish Academy's fifty-year rule information on the selection process for Pasternak became available for research in 2009. It is quite clear that the committee had long had him in their sights. The sudden appearance of a poorly produced error-ridden pirated edition of his novel barely a month before their announcement was due could not have had a determining influence on their decision. Anna Sergeyeva-Klyatis has examined the evidence thoroughly and critically. The most active supporter of Pasternak was Anders Österling, who would carry on being on the committee for sixty years and its chairman for almost twenty-five years. To substantiate Pasternak's candidature, Österling added two and a half pages to the reports already existing on him, asserting that he should become the main contender without the need for further discussion. He also submitted an article he had written on *Doctor Zhivago*, and which had been published in *Stockholms-Tidningen*, on 27th January 1958, long before the appearance of the pirated edition. The article was entitled 'Boris Pasternak's Novel about the Revolution.'

His recommendation to his fellow committee members made it clear that the fact that the work was not readily available in Russian need not affect their decision: '…in this case the Academy can make their decision with a clear conscience on the basis of the translation, disregarding the fact that the work has not yet been published by the Soviets'.[39]

In an article in *Pravda* on 10th November 2001, one of Pasternak's sons, Yevgeny Borisovich Pasternak, recalled how much stress his father had suffered long before the actual announcement of the award. Rumour had long been rife, and his position was insecure. Yevgeny reported that rumours were spreading immediately after the Second World War was over, and that the head of the Nobel Committee in 2001, Lars Gillensten, had confirmed that his nomination had been discussed every year from 1946 to 1950, then again in 1957, and it was finally awarded the following year in 1958. A simple check of the Nobel Nomination Database confirms the first of these assertions. Cecil M. Bowra, the literary historian at Oxford University, had nominated him in three of those years. In the other two (1948 and 1950) he had been nominated by Martin Lamm, a Swedish author and member of the Swedish Academy. Yevgeny reports that his father had guessed about such rumours rather than heard them himself. He had deduced it from the growing criticism of him by USSR official bodies. His son quoted him as saying that the Union of Soviet Writers was criticizing the fact that the West considered his work unusually important.

Clear evidence of the rumours came to him however in 1954 in a letter from his cousin in Leningrad (now St Petersburg), the authoress Olga Friedenberg. According to Yevgeny she wrote: 'There's a rumour here that you've received the Nobel Prize. Is it true? Otherwise, why such rumours?'[40] The translation of Pasternak's reply, as published on the pravda.ru website is generally unidiomatic, but the gist is as follows: he confirmed having heard the rumours himself and expressed fear that they might be true; he also reminded her that this might not mean he would be allowed to travel to the West, and even if he were he would not be able to 'act as usual talking doll' on such a trip. By this he meant presumably that he would not be able to stick to saying only what the Soviet government wanted him to say. He had heard another rumour that the nomination had been announced by the BBC, but that the Nobel Committee had waited first for Swedish government approval. The government, it appeared, preferred the committee to select Mikhail Sholokhov instead. It has not been possible to substantiate this rumour, which, if true, would reflect badly on the committee's concern to maintain political impartiality. It is to be hoped that it was an awareness of this which made them stick to their guns.

The morning after Pasternak received the telegram from the Nobel Prize Committee secretary, Anders Esterling, he had a visit from the author and party loyalist, Konstantin Fedin, who, according to Yevgeny's account, barged straight into Pasternak's room demanding that he make a clear and unambiguous refusal of the award, or the state media would persecute him. Pasternak was not cowed and stated that as he had already sent his acceptance he could hardly go back on his word. Fedin insisted that Pasternak accompany him immediately to his own summerhouse, where the head of the Cultural Department of the Party Central Committee was waiting to hear Pasternak's account of how the award had come about. But again Pasternak would not do as required.

Yevgeni remembered that his father was obviously pleased at receiving the award and had said that he 'would go through any deprivations for the honour of becoming a Nobel Laureate'.[41] Eventually he wrote to the Writers, Union defending his attitude and his work. Yevgeni tried hard to find the letter or a copy of it in the archives of the Writers' Union, but concluded that it must have been destroyed. His father told him about it in detail however, and he could remember that it contained twenty-two points, the most significant of which he explained in his article in *Pravda*: his father had agreed to alter all the unacceptable passages; he believed that the award was not for *Doctor Zhivago* alone but for the whole body of his work, as he had been nominated many times before the book's publication; under no circumstances would he decline the honour, though he was prepared to donate the money to a specific good cause; he was quite prepared to be dismissed from the Writers' Union, but warned them that they might well have to rehabilitate him in the course of time. But by the end of October he had given up his defiant attitude. It is unlikely that the KGB threat to arrest him would have been sufficient to bring this about, but they also talked of having Olga Ivinskaya dismissed and sent back to the gulag. On the 29th he phoned Olga and then sent his second telegram to the Nobel Committee. He sent another telegram to the Central Committee of the Communist party, to inform them that he had declined the award and to request that Olga be reinstated in her job. Yevgeny wrote that he could not recognize his father when he saw him that same evening. He mentioned his 'pale, lifeless face, tired painful eyes'. He said to his son 'Now it all doesn't matter, I declined the prize.'[42]

Despite his decision to decline the prize, members of the Writers' Union continued to denounce Pasternak in the press, and he was threatened formally with exile to the West. He felt that his writing was very much bound up with his Russian heritage, and eventually he wrote directly to the Soviet Premier, Nikita Khrushchev, explaining that to leave his motherland would be like a death sentence to him. Even the Prime Minister of India, Jawaharlal Nehru interceded on his behalf. The result was that exile never came about.

It is clear that Pasternak never really recovered his health after the stress incurred by the Nobel Prize affair, dying of lung cancer in May 1960. He wrote a poem called 'The Nobel Prize' which was published in English in the British weekly magazine *The New Statesman* in 1959. In the poem he asked the question whether he had behaved like a common criminal or murderer.

The American cartoonist Bill Mauldin expressed a similar idea in a cartoon which won for him the Pulitzer Prize for Editorial Cartooning in 1959. Two decrepit figures are shown working together in a wind-swept labour camp. One says to the other 'I won the Nobel Prize for literature. What was your crime?'

It would seem therefore wise for the Swedish Academy to attach a sticker to the back of the Nobel Prize medal: 'Government Warning: This prize can seriously damage your health.'

The Russians are Coming/not Coming

There have of course been other Russian laureates apart from Pasternak but he was the only one forced into a position in which he felt he had no option but to refuse. One could just as well have included him in the present chapter. But by pairing him with Sartre it is possible to consider the extremes of the spectrum of conditions under which a would-be laureate might think of refusing the honour. At one end of this spectrum, Sartre protests the freedom of the individual against all attempts to fit him into a hierarchy of values; and at the other end Pasternak is forced by a totalitarian hierarchy to decline for his own safety and that of others. Other Russian laureates have been in different kinds of relationships with the Soviet authorities. Ivan Bunin, Mikhail Sholokhov, Aleksandr Solzhenitsyn, and Joseph Brodsky all accepted but the circumstances of each case were unique.

The First Exile, or Tradition Diluted

Ivan Bunin, the first Russian to receive the prize, was living as an exile in France at the time of the award in 1933. He thus did not have to face the kind of pressure that was later to be put on Pasternak. Although he had travelled much in earlier years, his real emigration began in 1921. Before that he had already established a literary reputation. He came from a long line of rural gentry with Polish roots. His first poem was published when he was seventeen in 1887 and his first short story in 1891. He pursued various careers for a while, including working as a government clerk, librarian, court statistician and assistant editor. In 1895 he visited Moscow for the first time, and it is then that he became acquainted with many leading literary figures, such as Anton Chekhov, Maxim Gorky and Leo Tolstoy. Over the following decade he published poetry and stories which firmly established his reputation, and in 1909 he was elected as a member of the Russian Academy. By 1917 he had lost all faith in the various political movements in Russia and in April of that year he broke off his friendship with the pro-revolutionary Gorky. By 1919 he was working as the editor of the cultural section of the anti-Bolshevik newspaper *Iuzhnoe Slovo*. It was hatred of Bolshevism that finally made him decide to leave Russia and settle in France in 1921.

Bunin's diaries of the years 1918–20 started to appear under the title *Cursed Days* in 1925–6 in the Paris-based Russian newspaper *Vizrozhdenye*. The tone was strongly anti-Bolshevik and critical of all utopian visions. In the 1920s and 1930s Bunin thus became the revered spokesman for all Russian expatriates, especially for the writers among them. When the Swedish Academy honoured him with the Nobel Prize in 1933, it is easy to understand why this was regarded in Russia as a political act, the result of imperialist intrigue. It has been argued that an international prize has inevitably political dimensions, but the Swedish Academy claims that it has always taken great pains to make sure that its decisions have been free of political bias.[43]

Per Hallström, in his Presentation Speech to Bunin, avoided all direct reference to the Russian government of the day, though by focusing on him as heir to the classical Russian literary traditions implied that he owed little to contemporary aesthetic ideology. He was careful not to mention the Soviet Union by name: 'Thus he continued the art of the great realists while his contemporaries devoted themselves to the adventures of literary programs: symbolism, neo-naturalism, Adamism, futurism, and other names of such passing phenomena. He remained an isolated man in an extremely agitated era.'[44] He came closest to mentioning the threat of Bolshevism in his comments on Bunin's novel, *The Village*, of 1910, which 'made him famous and indeed notorious'.[45] In this work Bunin 'attacked the essential point of the Russian faith in the future, the Slavophiles' dream of the virtuous and able peasant, through whom the nation must someday cover the world with its shadow.'[46] And there is another implied criticism of contemporary Russian attitudes to literature in Hallström's comments on the work *Mitya's Love*, of 1924–5: 'The book was very successful in his country, although it signalled the return to literary traditions which, with many other things, had seemed condemned to death.'[47]

It is clear from this and other sources however that the Swedish Academy was concerned to reward according to traditional literary values rather than make a direct critique of socialist aesthetic values. Kjell Espmark's account (see Select Bibliography) of the discussions on Bunin confirm this. He had already been under consideration in 1931, when the committee stressed in its report that they had failed to find in Bunin's work 'any great or rich creative power, nor any irresistible or compelling narrative gift, nor any characters who in our imagination take on an intense personal life…'[48] And in the report of 1932 it was asserted that Bunin continued the tradition of great Russian narrative 'only in a somewhat diluted manner'.[49] The committee also complained that the translations they had read had not given them a sufficient sense of the style with which he was credited by fellow Russians. That he was finally given the award in 1933 was very much due to the efforts of his main supporter on the committee, Anders Österling, who provided convincing arguments for his artistry. Espmark notes that in making the award the Academy was very much making good their omissions in honouring exponents of the great Russian narrative tradition in the past, whom it was now too late to reward.[50]

Further confirmation that the Academy was acknowledging and rewarding a man they perceived to be the last surviving representative of a lost tradition is to be found in the Nobel Banquet speeches delivered in the Grand Hotel, Stockholm, on 10th December 1933. In his own speech Bunin clearly appreciated, or wished it to appear that he appreciated, that the award was being made by 'the most competent and impartial of juries'.[51] He also made a significant point that will be returned to in consideration of other laureates: 'For the first time since the founding of the Nobel Prize you have awarded it to an exile. Who am I in truth? An exile enjoying the hospitality of France...'[52] It is interesting to note that he prefers the term exile to émigré. And it is here that the political implications of his status become clear, if they are not described as such: 'It is necessary that there should be centres of absolute independence in the world.'[53] Referring to his fellow diners he adds

> ...we are united by one truth, the freedom of thought and conscience; to this freedom we owe civilization. For us writers, especially, freedom is dogma and an axiom. Your choice, gentlemen of the Academy, has proved once more that in Sweden the love of liberty is truly a national cult.[54]

Bunin's speech had been preceded by some introductory remarks by Professor Wilhelm Nordenson of the Caroline Institute, who did not pull his punches so cautiously: 'You have given us the most valuable picture of Russian society as it once was, and well do we understand the feelings with which you must have seen the destruction of the society with which you were so intimately connected. May our feelings of sympathy be of some comfort to you in the melancholy of exile.'[55]

It would seem from Espmark's account that the committee had not been especially enthusiastic about Bunin in the years prior to the award. But if the committee had not considered consciously the political situation in his home country which had driven him into exile, Österling had nevertheless somehow caught their conscience. There was clearly strong sympathy for the lonely free individual living in exile who represented the last of a dying breed.

Realist and Idealist, or a Communist with Heart

If there had been such a brouhaha over Pasternak in 1958, why, seven years later, did Mikhail Sholokhov escape a whipping, when he won the prize? Was it simply that Sholokhov had not provoked the government in any way? Was he considered by the Writers' Union to be the acceptable face of Soviet Literature? However these questions are answered, they demonstrate the undeniable political dimensions of the award. Whatever the intentions of the Swedish Academy, the rest of the world will choose what shade of political spin to put on the decision. And try as they may to remain politically neutral, many of the statements made by individual members of the Nobel Committee have revealed their political biases.

The problem from the committee's perspective, and as Espmark explains it[56], is that in many countries in which cultural organizations are under the direct control of the government, it is difficult for politicians and ordinary people alike to imagine that an award by one country to a writer in another country could be anything other than a political act. They fail, Espmark argues, to perceive that the Swedish Academy is an autonomous body, able to conduct its business entirely without interference from state or government. Thus there came about the extraordinary misunderstanding in the case of the Russian Premier Nikita Khrushchev's claim that he was personally responsible for ensuring that Sholokhov was awarded the Nobel Prize.

Khrushchev claimed in his memoirs that he had advised the Academy, via a Swedish minister, to give the prize to Sholokhov. Press coverage at the time in Sweden was based on the assumption that the leak was proven, and that the Academy had indeed yielded to Khrushchev's pressure. When Khrushchev's claim was made known, the Academy member Lars Gyllensten deemed it necessary to clear their name in an article in the newspaper *Dagens Nyheter* (27th February 1984). He stressed the fact that the various Swedish academies are 'private associations, and freedom from political control is for them an affair of the heart' and that 'avoiding the influence of political powers is axiomatic'.[57] Then he addressed directly Khrushchev's claim: 'the prize to Sholokhov may have been wise or unwise – Nikita Khrushchev has neither honor nor blame with regard to the fact that it was given.'[58]

In fact Sholokhov had long been under consideration by the committee. Espmark writes that he had been a serious competitor to Pasternak since 1947. But Pasternak had gained more favour among the committee members and was given priority for both his poetic qualities and the psychological insights of his prose. Sholokhov would have to wait, Espmark writes in words of disturbing ambiguity and belying the Academy's claim to complete neutrality, 'until the time was ripe for a new Russian prize.'[59]

Of course thoughts about the world political situation could not be blocked out completely from the minds of the academicians. Nor would one expect such intelligent men to be insensitive to the context in which they were awarding the prize. The member Dag Hammarskjöld had realized back in the mid-fifties what international reaction might ensue and had clearly wanted to avoid it. At that time his mind had been clearly torn between going ahead regardless and avoiding a furore. On 12th May 1955, he had written to Sten Selander about Sholokhov: 'I would vote against Sholokhov based not only on artistic grounds and not only as an automatic response to attempts to pressure us but also on the ground that a prize to a Soviet author today, involving as it would the kind of political motivations that would readily be alleged, is to me an idea with very little to recommend it.'[60]

Thus finally, in 1965, 'the time was ripe' for Sholokhov. Even in the preliminary round of voting, eight of the thirteen members voted for him. It is interesting to note that in the award ceremony speech by Anders Österling, there is but a brief mention of Sholokhov's more recent work, with the main focus on his earlier masterpiece, known in English as *And Quiet Flows the Don*, which took him fourteen years to complete between 1926 and 1940. Of the rest of his works only a recent one is mentioned briefly in one sentence: *Virgin Soil Upturned*, written between 1932 and 1959, a novel about the compulsory collectivization of farms in Russia. In his speech Österling revealed that the committee was only too aware that many in Russia might be uncomfortable with their choice, especially as it was based on that one particular work. Rather than ignore the matter and attempt to sweep it under the carpet, he decided to provide public recognition of what everyone knew to be the case in Russia, as though to underline that the committee had made its choice purely on literary grounds. The work had been '...long viewed with some concern by the Soviet critics, whose political affiliation made it difficult for them to accept, wholeheartedly, Sholokhov's quite natural commitment to his theme, that of the Cossacks' revolt against the new central authorities; nor could they easily accept...the defiant spirit of independence...'[61]

Österling mentions Sholokhov's political allegiance, only to stress that it played no manifest role in the novel under consideration, nor, by implication, in the committee's deliberations: 'Although a convinced Communist, Sholokhov keeps ideological comment out of his book completely...'[62]

The official brief biography written at the time of the award, and available on the Nobel Prize website, clearly recognized Sholokhov as a pillar of Soviet society: 'In 1932 Sholokhov joined the Communist Party and, on several occasions, has been a delegate of the Soviet Academy of Sciences and later vice president of the Association of Soviet Writers.'[63]

In the light of this, the Soviet government's decision to allow Sholokhov to attend the award ceremony and receive his prize is not surprising. However anyone in the West might interpret it, it could be presented to the Russian people as international recognition of the highest achievements of Soviet culture. Whether or not Khrushchev had any influence, the effect he desired came about. There can be no doubt that Sholokhov himself was very much aware how important the event was to his government. The word 'soviet' was very carefully emphasized by him in his Banquet Speech: 'I am proud that this prize has been awarded to a Russian, a Soviet writer.'[64]

In the same speech he defended the realist tradition of novel-writing against modern experiments. It was new content and not new form that was needed: 'In my opinion the true pioneers are those who make manifest in their works the new content, the determining characteristics of life in our time...'[65] Though he did not employ the term directly he was clearly concerned to indicate that his work was in accordance with the 'ideal direction' stipulated by Nobel and for the general benefit of mankind. He also managed to slip in, indirectly, a reference to the aesthetic ideology of the Soviet Union. He thus attempted to placate both the Swedish Academy and the Supreme Soviet within the scope of two sentences: 'I am speaking of a realism that carries within itself the concept of life's regeneration, its reformation for the benefit of mankind. I refer, of course, to the realism we describe as socialist.'[66] Throughout the speech in fact he managed to express his humanism in terms which were compatible with both the ideals of Alfred Nobel and those of communism.

In his introductory remarks Karl Ragnar Gierow had been equally diplomatic in stressing Sholokhov's humanism rather than his socialism. The author's subject was, he claimed, 'The human heart, which is the real battlefield of all victories and defeats that befall this earth of ours.'[67]

Smuggling the Truth, or Four Years
in the Life of Aleksandr Isayevich

The occasion of Aleksandr Isayevich Solzhenitsyn being awarded
the Nobel Prize in 1970 became a cause célèbre indeed and provided the one controversy involving the prize that most people
have heard of, even if they have heard little else about it. Officially
he was given the prize for 'the ethical force with which he has
pursued the indispensable traditions of Russian literature'.[68]
Now the Swedish Academy has always chosen its words extremely carefully and taken care also to translate them accurately.
One must have sympathy for them: locked in a never-ending
struggle to reinterpret the wording of Nobel's will anew for each
succeeding generation. The expression 'ethical force,' as difficult
as it may be to define precisely, does convey the image of a man
who, with great and indefatigable determination, always did
what he thought was right. It is undoubtedly this very characteristic trait which became the motor driving the whole crisis sur-
rounding the award made to him. And 'indispensable traditions'?
Indispensable to whom? Not particularly to the West, but certainly to the Russian people: they should know every ghastly
detail of the atrocities committed in the name of Soviet-style
socialism. And thus indispensable to humanity in general. Crimes
against humanity became his subject matter.

The choice of Solzhenitsyn had not always been a foregone
conclusion however. Espmark has argued that by the late 1960s
there was evidence that some new blood was being added to
the Academy. While Österling was still playing an important
role, Karl Ragnar Gierow took over as chairman in 1970, and the
initiative was being taken mainly by younger members, such
as Lars Gyllensten, Artur Lundkvist and Johannes Edfelt. But
despite the changes there was an undeniable continuity in the
priorities which the committee pursued in their selection
process: they were looking for 'pioneers', writers who were
attempting to renew the genres in which they wrote. Already in

1962 Lundkvist had criticized the choice of John Steinbeck as 'one of its greatest mistakes' because he had shown little evidence that his work provided 'the *renewal* of narrative fiction'.[69] When the prize was given to Solzhenitsyn in 1970 Lundkvist objected along similar lines.

Public opinion of the selection of Solzhenitsyn seemed to be that it had been a political decision. Lundkvist denied this in an interview (in *Aftonbladet*, 10th December 1970), saying 'All prizes are political in their effect, if not in their intention.'[70] When the interview was published it bore the headline 'It was Politics That Gave Solzhenitsyn the Prize.' In fact, and not surprisingly, the press played a significant role in stirring up all the hype around the event, as they were to do later with controversial decisions. As is so often the case however, the press, for the most part, did not base its accusations on adequate research. There was, and still is, a general lack of awareness of the fact that proposal and award were rarely the work of one year. Individual writers are discussed for many years before it is decided that their time has come. Thus although there had been a well-organised campaign in the Swedish press in support of Solzhenitsyn, this had had no bearing, according to the member Kjell Strömberg[71], on the committee's deliberations. When the announcement was finally made, the Russian state press also entered the fray. On 9th October, *TASS* (the state news agency) reported the claim by the Writers' Union that the decision had been politically motivated: 'It is regrettable that the Swedish Academy has allowed itself to be drawn into an unworthy spectacle that was staged not at all to advance the spiritual values and traditions of literature but was dictated by speculative political considerations.'[72] On 14th October, the *Literaturnaya Gazeta* accused the Nobel Committee of having yielded to the pressure of international journalists and of a particular Russian exile publication. Despite all this, Espmark, who researched the archive thoroughly on this, as other matters, asserts that there is no evidence that the committee or the Academy expected that there would be such a political backlash.[73]

In fact they were concerned to do as much as possible to avoid such a backlash. There is evidence that one member of the committee attempted to check first if there might be any political repercussions. This suggests two things: that there was some anxiety about it and that they wanted to reduce political repercussions to a minimum. The then Swedish ambassador in Moscow, Gunnar Jarring, wrote in his memoirs that he had received a letter from Gierow enquiring about possible effects on Solzhenitsyn personally, not about any broader political consequences. Jarring was able to reassure him that there were signs that the Russian government was not taking punitive measures against scientists and scholars whose works had been published abroad.

However Jarring also wrote separately to the Academy to urge them to postpone their decision for several years, as the award would lead to difficulties in relations between the Swedish Foreign Office and the Soviet Union. But the committee refused to let itself be swayed by such considerations.[74]

Before examining aspects of the Presentation Speech for Solzhenitsyn, his Banquet speech and Nobel Lecture, there is a story to be told about how it all came about which is worthy of a John Le Carré novel. The gist of this is recounted in an essay by Stig Fredrikson, included on the official Nobel website, with the enticing title: 'How I Helped Alexander Solzhenitsyn Smuggle his Nobel Lecture from the USSR.'[75]

There were professional and personal reasons why Solzhenitsyn decided not to go to Stockholm in December 1970 to receive the prize. He had been expelled from the Writers' Union and harassed by the KGB, and had good reason to believe that if he went to Sweden he would be deprived of his Soviet citizenship. Thus he would be prevented from going back to his homeland, which provided material and motivation for all his writing. His wife Natalya was also expecting a child.

What happened next was not one of the most glorious episodes in the history of the Swedish Academy, nor of the

Swedish government, and it left Solzhenitsyn feeling humiliated and angry.

Ambassador Jarring and the Swedish government, together with Prime Minister Olof Palme, attempted to arrange for a ceremony to take place in the Swedish Embassy in Moscow, at which Solzhenitsyn would be presented with the prize. Friends and other guests approved by Solzhenitsyn would be invited and he would hold his lecture there. Solzhenitsyn was angry and described the conditions imposed as 'an insult to the Nobel Prize itself' and suggested that it seemed as though the prize was something to be ashamed of, something to be concealed from the people.'[76]

When Stig Fredrikson arrived in Moscow early in 1972 (two years after the original award), as a correspondent for several Scandinavian news agencies, he learned of another plan. The Permanent Secretary, Gierow, was to hand over the prize to Solzhenitsyn in his wife's apartment. The source for this information, Fredrikson's editor, would seem to be reliable: his name was Hans Björkegren; he was also Solzhenitsyn's Swedish translator and handled the practical arrangements for the ceremony. Solzhenitsyn was actually forbidden to register as a resident of Moscow, so that Natalya's address had to be kept a secret. Fredrikson was informed of it by Björkegren. Everything was arranged to take place on 9th April 1972, which was Easter Sunday by the Orthodox calendar. Then suddenly there was an insuperable hitch: Gierow was refused a visa to Russia, and the ceremony had to be cancelled. Solzhenitsyn exploded with anger in a public letter in which he asked the Swedish Academy to 'keep the Nobel insignia for an indefinite period'.[77] Fredrikson reports however that Solzhenitsyn was still determined to deliver his Nobel Lecture. And it is from this point on that Fredrikson's report takes on the characteristics of a spy thriller, with the difference that it is not fiction but the true account of the kind of subterfuge necessary in a totalitarian state.

Solzhenitsyn and Fredrikson agreed to meet again secretly in the underground passage at a railway station. Solzhenitsyn himself provides an evocative account of the meeting in his memoir *The Oak and the Calf* of 1975: 'I had in my pocket a film containing the text of the Nobel speech. We had failed to find any other way of sending it out, and once again, its destination was Sweden. I was standing in an inconspicuous spot. He and his wife Ingrid came strolling along arm in arm: I followed, keeping a gap between us, and Alya came behind me, after watching out for a while from a different spot to make sure that no one was tailing us. Everything turned out fine, so we caught up with them and the four of us set off at a leisurely pace down the Leningrad Prospect.'[78]

Fredrikson reports that when he returned to his own apartment that evening he examined carefully what Solzhenitsyn had given him: '...I had received nine black and white negatives wrapped in a paper envelope. I took a small transistor radio, unscrewed the back, took out the batteries, and in the empty space I placed the negatives. I had cut the negatives into strips, wrapped them up in plastic and put the roll in an empty tube of headache tablets. The tin tube fitted nicely in the battery space. I put the radio in my suitcase and took the train to Helsinki for a conference with my editors. Everything went smoothly at the border, and in Helsinki I could tell my editor Hans Björkegren that "I have mail for you from Moscow."'[79]

From Helsinki the film was taken directly to the Swedish Academy in Stockholm. It was published in both the Swedish and the international press in the summer of that year, 1972, and caused a worldwide sensation, especially for its first mention of the infamous 'Gulag Archipelago.'

The rest of Fredrikson's account is equally fascinating but not immediately relevant to the matter of the Nobel Prize. From that meeting in the underground passage dated Fredrikson's 'career as a secret courier to Solzhenitsyn'. It lasted for almost two years until Solzhenitsyn was arrested and sent into exile in February 1974. Fredrikson even managed to persuade the Norwegian embassy in Moscow to let him smuggle out films and documents in their diplomatic bag. He became an indispensable link for Solzhenitsyn to the West.

When Solzhenitsyn suspected that the KGB had somehow obtained a copy of *The Gulag Archipelago*, he became concerned that they would try to discredit him, and he gave a letter to Fredrikson which urged the speedy publication of at least the first volume in the West. Why the work would be such a bombshell was clear from the description of the book's contents given by Solzhenitsyn to Fredrikson as a small type-written press release: 'a documentary study in several volumes about the Soviet prison camps in the years 1918–56, based on evidence from more than 200 people who on different occasions spent time in the camps.'[80]

After several weeks of reviews in the international press condemning the Soviet Union, the Communist party newspaper *Pravda*, finally published an article, on 14th January 1974, describing Solzhenitsyn as a traitor. On 12th February, Solzhenitsyn was arrested in Natalya's apartment. The following day he was deprived of his Russian citizenship and sent into exile, stopping first in West Germany, where he was welcomed into the home of the 1972 Nobel Prizewinner in Literature, Heinrich Böll. On 10th December 1974, he was finally able to attend the Nobel Prize ceremony in Stockholm. He was to remain in exile until 1994.

Gierow had already prepared two speeches of presentation long before Solzhenitsyn was able to come to Stockholm to receive the Nobel insignia. On the latter occasion his remarks to Solzhenitsyn open with poignant words: 'I have already made two speeches to you. The first one you couldn't listen to, because there was a frontier to cross. The second one I couldn't deliver, because there was a frontier to cross.'[81]

In retrospect Gierow's original 1970 Presentation Speech contains statements which yield bitter irony after *Pravda*'s role in branding Solzhenitsyn a traitor and paving the way for his exile. The award was primarily for his novel *One Day in the Life of Ivan Denisovich*, first published in 1962 with the explicit personal approval of Nikita Khrushchev. In his 1970 speech, Gierow quoted the article in *Pravda* praising the work and comparing Solzhenitsyn to Tolstoy. The *Pravda* journalist asked why the novel makes the reader's spirit soar: 'The explanation lies in its profound humanity, in the quality of mankind even in the hour of degradation.'[82] It would have been very satisfying to have been able to fling those words back into the face of the editor of *Pravda* on the occasion of Solzhenitsyn's degradation.

In his Banquet Speech in 1974 to express his gratitude, Solzhenitsyn managed some words of wry humour: '...the Swedish Academy and the Nobel Foundation have probably never had as much bother with anyone as they have had with me.' And he added, 'Four years had to pass to give me the floor for three minutes.' He also provided some insight into the positive effects that the award of a prize like the Nobel Prize can have: 'It has prevented me from being crushed in the severe persecutions to which I have been subjected. It has helped my voice to be heard in places where my predecessors have not been heard for decades.' Although probably not consciously he also echoed the priority that the committee had given of late to evidence of a pioneering spirit: 'But perhaps the finest task of any literary or scientific prize is precisely to help clear the road ahead.' And he leapt to the defence of the Academy against accusations of political bias: 'We all know that an artist's work cannot be contained within the wretched dimension of politics.'[83]

The final irony in the Solzhenitsyn affair is that his Nobel Lecture, which shook the sleep of the world, was never actually read out. Thanks to Stig Fredrikson's efforts it was available to all, except of course to Soviet citizens, long before its author could visit Stockholm. A short note hidden away at the end of the online text of the lecture reminds the reader: 'Delivered only to the Swedish Academy and not actually given as a lecture.'[84]

In his Banquet Speech Solzhenitsyn admitted that he had been fully aware of what he was hitting the Academy with in his Nobel Lecture back in 1970, 'on the first free tribune of my life.'

It was his first chance to speak out about everything which weighed heavily on his mind: 'For a writer from a land without liberty, his first tribune and his first speech is a speech about everything in the world, about all the torments in his country…'[85]

It certainly feels to the reader of his lecture as though Solzhenitsyn is attempting to pour out everything he thinks and feels about 'everything in the world'. It is impossible and unfair to attempt a summary of it, but it ranges over art, archaeology, politics, truth, goodness and beauty, over globalization, East and West (compared and contrasted), norms of value and morality, history and forgetfulness, nationality and diversity, literature and power, the Chinese Cultural Revolution, suppression of information, science, and individual writers such as Dostoevsky, Camus and Böll, and last, but far from least, the Gulag Archipelago. All human life, as they say, is there. He is as open about his disillusionments as about his enthusiasms, so that the catchphrases of the socialism he grew up with (class struggle, struggle of the masses, etc.) are for him but 'respectable pseudonyms' for 'those same old cave-age emotions'[86] (what one might also call old whines in new bottles?).

'A View over Two Slopes', or Geographic Justice

Perhaps a more practical and less troublesome approach to getting the Nobel Prize is that of Joseph Brodsky [1987]: become an exile fairly early on in your career, so that you can give all your attention to developing a literary reputation, while being able to leave spaces in your calendar every year for a possible invitation to the Nobel Prize Ceremony and related press conferences.

Brodsky was born in 1940 in a Jewish family in Leningrad. The family was poor and nearly died of starvation in the Siege of Leningrad. He left school at fifteen and tried various jobs. He learned Polish and English and became familiar with the poetry written in those languages. In 1955 he began writing his own poetry and it was circulated in underground journals. In 1963 his poetry was denounced by a Leningrad newspaper as pornographic and anti-Soviet and he was put on trial in 1964. It was judged that his series of odd jobs and his writing poetry did not constitute a sufficient contribution to a socialist society. He was sentenced to five years' hard labour and spent eighteen months of it on a farm in the Archangel region. His sentence was commuted in 1965 after protests by prominent Soviet and foreign cultural figures, such as the poet Yevgeny Yevtushenko, the composer Shostakovich and the French philosopher Jean-Paul Sartre.

He returned to Leningrad and continued to write for another seven years, with most of his work being published abroad in foreign languages. In 1972 an official Soviet mental health expert, Andrei Snezhnevsky, diagnosed him as suffering from 'paranoid reformist delusion'. He was at first urged to emigrate to Israel but he refused. After his papers were confiscated he was put on a flight to Vienna on 4th June 1972. In Vienna he was helped by, among others, the British poet W.H. Auden, who would eventually help him to settle in America, where he stayed for the rest of his life. Although he was invited to return to Russia after the fall of the Soviet Union he never went back. In America he had an impressive career as a poet and academic, winning many awards. In 1991 he became the American Poet Laureate. He wrote in both Russian and English, translating his own works.

The Swedish Academy was clearly very much aware of the problematic aspects of deciding to award the prize to Brodsky in 1987, though they clearly also recognized the differences between his situation and those of Pasternak and Solzhenitsyn. There would be nothing to stop Brodsky from accepting the award and attending the ceremony, but it might of course provoke a negative reaction in Russia. Espmark has put it succinctly: 'The choice of a Soviet dissident, who could be recognized as one of our age's great poets only after he had begun his life of exile in the United States had political implications of which the Academy was naturally not unaware.'[87]

Perhaps because the laureate was safely installed in the West, Sture Allén, in his award ceremony speech, clearly felt that he could be more explicit about East/West differences, and the poet himself had made this a theme in his work: 'For him Russian and English are two attitudes to the world. Having both languages at one's disposal is like sitting on the top of an existential hill with a view over two slopes, over humanity's two tendencies of development, he has declared.' But Allén was concerned not to provide a one-sided criticism: 'The poet also becomes the spokesman in the totalitarian society's apparent silence and the open society's stupefying flood of information.'[88]

In his Banquet Speech Brodsky highlighted the irony of the fact that he had been born just on the other side of the Baltic but had had to travel via America to get to Stockholm on that day, 'but then for a man of my occupation the notion of a straight line being the shortest distance between two points has lost its attraction a long time ago. So it pleases me to find out that geography in its own turn is also capable of poetic justice.'[89]

Brodsky's Nobel Lecture is remarkable and memorable for the interspersion of witty aphorisms which drive home his points with greater conviction than impersonal pleas and logical analysis ever could. Even out of context they provoke and stimulate fresh lines of thought, and function thus as epigrams. A few quotations will have to suffice to inspire the would-be laureate:

...it is better to be a total failure in democracy than a martyr or the crème de la crème in tyranny.
...as long as the state permits itself to interfere with the affairs of literature, literature has the right to interfere with the affairs of state.
...in everyday life you can tell the same joke thrice and, thrice getting a laugh, become the life of the party. In art, though, this sort of conduct is called 'cliché'.[90]

He distinguishes between literature and literacy. Literature is humanizing, but you can be literate and still kill your fellow human beings: 'Lenin was literate, Stalin was literate, so was Hitler; as for Mao Zedong, he even wrote verse. What all these men had in common, though, was that their hit list was longer than their reading list.'[91]

One final gem from his lecture gives us further food for thought: '...in a real tragedy, it is not the hero who perishes; it is the chorus.'[92] Worthy of Bertolt Brecht, that one.

Chips off the Old Bloc?

Of course it was not only the Russians who had problems getting across the Baltic to Stockholm. Throughout much of the twentieth century prior to the collapse of the Soviet Union, many of Russia's satellite states were either directly under the all-too-watchful eyes of the leadership in Moscow or had repressive regimes of their own, which frowned with various degrees of severity on dissent.

Poles Apart

There are few literary laureates from the area loosely defined as Eastern Europe prior to the Soviet Union's period of most extensive influence after the Second World War (the Soviet Union can be dated from its treaty of creation in 1922 till its dissolution in the late 1980s). One of the very earliest laureates was in fact a Pole, Henryk Sienkiewicz, in 1905. In the Presentation Speech he was praised by Wirsén for his evocation of 'the spirit of the nation',[93] and in his Banquet Speech Sienkiewicz himself saw the prize as being awarded not to him personally '…but to the Polish achievement, the Polish genius.'[94] It was a time when nationalism was rife and regarded positively throughout Europe.

Wirsén also pointed out that Sienkiewicz had been greatly admired for his sense of history and that among those who had nominated him there had been several eminent historians. His novels ranged from the world of the Teutonic Knights to life in the seventeenth century, but the one work which made him internationally famous, and which is probably the only one of his works many people can name today, was *Quo Vadis*. He wrote it over the years 1895 to 1896, and it had already been translated into more than thirty languages before the Nobel award ceremony. The novel tells the history of the persecution of Christians under the Roman emperor Nero. And Wirsén drew attention to the fact that the novel had sold 800,000 copies within one year in England and America alone. Whether his idealized vision of Christianity contrasted with what Wirsén called 'gangrened paganism' could attract him as many readers today is another question.

Then, in 1924, it was the turn of another Polish author, Władysław Reymont, to win the prize. He had witnessed major changes in his country and in Russia, but died, in 1925, before the worst excesses of Nazism and Stalinism were to break upon the world. In the latter part of his life he had however been aware of the growth of Bolshevism and had lived through the establishment of the Soviet Union in 1922. Poland had also gone to war with Russia between 1919 and 1922. The prize was awarded primarily for his novel *The Peasants*, published over several years from 1904 to 1909, but he also published much travel writing and many short stories. There are two works which have similar titles when translated into English, but should not be confused. There was the trilogy of novels written between 1911 and 1917 on the French Revolution of 1794. In Polish it is called *Rok 1794*, and *'rok'* has been variously translated as 'revolution' or 'revolt'. Then there is his last novel, serialized in 1922 and published in book form in 1924, entitled *Bunt*, which has also been translated as 'revolt' or 'insurrection'. It portends of what this politically aware author might have produced had he not died of heart disease at the age of fifty-eight. The novel appeared during the period when Joseph Stalin was consolidating his power in the Soviet

Union, becoming General Secretary of the Communist Party of the Soviet Union in April 1922. By the end of the 1920s Russia was a totalitarian state.

Reymont's novel not only satirized the Soviet Union mercilessly but prefigured another universally renowned work of satire by more than twenty years: George Orwell's *Animal Farm*, published in 1945. The similarities between the concepts of both novels are so close that it is difficult not to surmise that Orwell may well have known about Reymont's novel, even if he had not actually read it. There is however no known reference to Reymont's work in anything written by Orwell. In Reymont's novel the animals on a farm revolt and attempt to establish a society in which the watchword is 'equality', but freedoms are soon abused and a new totalitarian 'state' is set up which rules by terror.

Reymont's novel was banned in communist-dominated Poland from 1945 to 1989, as was Orwell's *Animal Farm*.

The Cold Sets In

The Bosnian Serbo-Croat

In 1961, when the Cold War was still as chilly as ever, the Swedish Academy awarded the prize to the 'Yugoslav' novelist, Ivo Andrić. There is good reason for enclosing his nationality in inverted commas as will soon become obvious. Analysing the post-war period of the prize, Espmark judges Andrić to be one of those 'regional figures who could have achieved a worldwide public only through the prize'.[9]

Whatever his literary merits, Andrić was not a writer who was likely to ruffle any feathers, politically speaking, either east or west. He was a diplomat who wrote mainly about the culture, folklore and history of his native area, and in that area renowned for its ethnic strife, he was championed by each ethnic and linguistic group as their own.

A quick survey can convey the complexity of the man's identity. He was born in 1892 to Croatian parents in Bosnia. After a period as diplomat in various European countries, he spent the Second World War in Belgrade, Serbia, working on the novels that made him famous. He obtained various posts in the Communist government of Yugoslavia, and became a parliamentary representative for Bosnia and Herzegovina. Claims have been made for him variously as a Serbian, Croatian and Bosnian author. He had enrolled in Jagiellonian University, Kraków, Poland, as a Croat in 1914, but his Yugoslav identity card issued in 1951 declares him to be a Serb. He wrote in what is generally known as the Serbo-Croatian language, but used different dialects of that language at various stages of his writing career. When he married Milica Babić at the age of sixty-seven in 1958, he declared himself to be a Serb. The Swedish Academy, in its wisdom, has settled for 'Residence at the time of the award: Yugoslavia' and 'Language: Serbo-Croatian.'

The only time Andrić really fell foul of authority for political activities was when he was imprisoned during the First World War by the Austrian government. After the Second World War he gradually became a respected member of the establishment. When he won the Nobel Prize he donated all the money to the improvement of libraries in Bosnia and Herzegovina. He also became a member of the Serbian Academy of Sciences and Arts.

In his Banquet Speech Andrić interpreted the award as being not so much for his own achievements as a writer but rather as an encouragement to his whole country in its cultural endeavours: '… that country's literature is beginning to gain recognition through an honest endeavour to make its contribution to world literature. There is no doubt that your distinction of a writer of this country is an encouragement which calls for our gratitude.'[96]

In the speech Andrić focuses mainly on the nature of storytelling and especially on the use of historical subjects. His credo should stand as sound advice to writers who would emulate him:

In the end it matters little whether the writer evokes the past, describes the present, or even plunges boldly into the future. The main thing is the spirit which informs his story, the message that his work conveys to mankind; and it is obvious that rules and regulations do not avail here. Each builds his story according to his own inward needs, according to the measure of his inclinations, innate or acquired, according to his conceptions and to the power of his means of expression. Each assumes the moral responsibility for his own story and each must be allowed to tell it freely.[97]

Poetry as Refuge and Opposition

The Czech Jaroslav Seifert [1984] was a poet who managed to openly oppose a state's oppressive regime while at the same time having his works published and recognized in that state. In his award-ceremony speech Lars Gyllensten emphasized his significance and importance within his own country, stressing that he had published almost thirty volumes of poems over a period of more than sixty years. When he was young Seifert supported the ideals of socialist revolution and wrote poems on the subject. The ideals of his youth explain the opposition of his maturity. Gyllensten summarizes these ideals with the words 'The state is there for the people and not vice versa.'[98] In his youth he had hoped for a world in which war and oppression would be abolished, but after the devastating historical events which swept over Europe in the 1930s and 1940s his poetry took on a darker tone.

Gyllensten also points out that the post-war period in Czechoslovakia also proved to be a great disappointment for Seifert. He refused to follow the aesthetic ideals of socialist realism which essentially forced him to put his art in the service of political propaganda. One of the most notable public demonstrations of his opposition to the regime and its cultural policy was his signing of the so-called 'Charter 77'. On 6th January 1977, a manifesto called the 'Charter 77' appeared first in West German newspapers, before being distributed around the world. This was a declaration by various notable people concerned about the protection of civil and general human rights in Czechoslovakia. It was basically a demand that the Czech government respect rights which were guaranteed in the constitution but in practice were not being respected. Among the signatories were various prominent Czech figures, including many in the arts and public affairs. By the end of the year 1977 it had over 800 signatures and by 1985 about 1,200. The government of Gustáv Husák was furious. A large number of the signatories were arrested, interrogated and in many cases dismissed from their posts.

In 1984, when Seifert was awarded the Nobel Prize there was only scant reporting of it in the government-controlled state media. He had become *persona non grata*. Gyllensten points out that in his writing Seifert managed to attack the principles embodied in the Husák regime without naming it specifically and mainly by presenting a contrasting ideology. When Gyllensten uses the innocent word 'spring' he is clearly alluding to a specific political 'spring' readily identifiable by his audience with historical events in the city of Prague: 'He praises a Prague that is blossoming and a spring that lives in the memory, in the hopes or the defiant spirit of people who refuse to conform.'[99]

Seifert was unable to attend the Nobel Banquet and his speech was read by his daughter. He died two years later at the age of eighty-six. His Nobel Lecture was about the role of poetry in the history and culture of the Czech people and about the lyrical state of mind in general. What he wrote confirms what Gyllensten had said on his views on poetry: 'Since the war... poetry has occupied a very important position in our cultural life. It is as though poetry lyrics were predestined not only to speak to people very closely, extremely intimately, but also to be our deepest and safest refuge, where we seek succour in adversities we sometimes dare not even name.' And a little later he adds: 'There are countries and nations that find their questions and the answers to them expressed by wise and perceptive thinkers. Sometimes, journalists and mass media perform that role. With us, it is as though our national spirit, in attempting to find embodiment, chose poets and made them its spokesmen.' He argues also that poetry is a particularly suitable medium of opposition in a country such as his and perhaps the only effective one. It is suitable because of 'its ability to merely suggest, to use allusion, metaphor, to express what is central in a veiled manner, to conceal from unauthorized eyes.'[100]

Espmark draws attention to the view expressed in some parts of the press, especially the Swedish press, that the choice of Seifert was undoubtedly politically motivated and implied criticism of the Czech government and support for Czech writers and the Czech people. His opinion is best summed up in his own words: '...in making the choice the Academy was clearly aware of the political implications of Seifert's work, but that is different from saying such an awareness determined the result.'[101]

The Man from Nowhere

Czesław Milosz [1980], like Bunin in 1933, produced most of his work in voluntary exile, and in his Nobel Lecture he presented some perceptive insights into the situation of the exiled writer. He thus leads us very conveniently to the next area of focus in the present study.

He was born in 1911 in a country, Lithuania, which at the time of the award no longer existed as an independent state. The press release by the Swedish Academy makes a point of emphasizing this: 'This country and this culture, and most of its people, no longer exist. The Nazi terror and genocide, the war, and later, the Stalinistic tyranny, have wiped them out, in hardships exceeding what Poland and the Baltic States have suffered many times before.'[102] Milosz grew up in the Polish town of Vilnius and was educated there. At first, after the Second World War, he supported the socialist regime and became cultural attaché for the government in Paris, but as Poland generally took a more distinctly Stalinist direction he felt that he could no longer represent it and defected in 1951, at first settling in Paris. In 1960 he moved to

America and became a lecturer on Polish literature at Berkeley University in California.

For Milosz, exile became a metaphor his whole existence, a point noted in the Nobel Prize press release: 'In both an inward and an outward sense, he is an exiled writer – a stranger for whom the physical exile is really a reflection of a metaphysical, or even religious, spiritual exile applying to humanity in general.'[103]

In his Banquet Speech, while considering his place in Polish literature as a literary exile, Milosz also recalls how in his life in Poland before exile, and especially in the Second World War, poetry came to be the only means of expression for many. There are echoes here of the views of his fellow lyricist, Jaroslav Seifert. Milosz also clearly felt that, by attending the award ceremony, he was representing the voiceless masses who had suffered and died: 'Lines of Polish verse circulated underground, were written in barracks of concentration camps and in soldiers' tents in Asia, Africa, and Europe. To represent here such a literature is to feel humble before testimonies of love and heroic self-sacrifice left by those who are no more.'[104]

When the choice of Milosz for the prize was formally announced there was the familiar discussion in some quarters about whether it had been politically motivated. Espmark cites several journalists who raised the question. The suspicion was that somehow Poland was in fashion. The Academy member Artur Lundkvist was asked in an interview in the British newspaper *The Sunday Times* whether the Polish general strike in Danzig had really had no influence on the decision, and Lundkvist replied that Milosz had already been under consideration for three or four years and had been shortlisted in May 1980. This was long before the famous Danzig strike.[105]

The reaction in Moscow was strong and predictable. In *Literaturnaya Gazeta* Milosz was described as 'a rather middling poet and a bitter anticommunist'. He had been given the award 'precisely for his anticommunist stance'.[106] To Espmark ('one who has had the opportunity to study the documents') the accusation was absurd. He has pointed out how Gyllensten, in his award-ceremony speech was especially careful to stress those aspects of the writer that were in accordance with 'the humanistic tradition of the Nobel Prize in Literature'. Espmark concludes his reflections on the case of Milosz with one of his most vehement attacks on the credo of socialist realism: 'Justifying a prize by focusing on not only an author's interpretation of the human predicament but his integrity is quite simply beyond the grasp of Marxist-Leninist aesthetics, which interprets such a focus as mere camouflage for political intentions.'[107]

In Exile, or Home Thoughts from Abroad

The Search for a Habitable Land

Heinrich Böll might seem to be an odd starting point for a consideration of laureates who found themselves by chance or of necessity in exile, since he spent most of his life within his home country of Germany, but in his Banquet Speech on the occasion of receiving the prize in 1972, he focused on the plight of the author in exile and saw close connections between exiles and refugees, or *Vertriebene*,[108] those who have been driven away from their homes. The German word suggests the negative rather than the optimistic aspect of the phenomenon, 'driven away' rather than 'seeking refuge'.[109]

Böll had experienced at first hand the suffering of people driven from their homes in the latter stages of the Second World War: '...there were always refugees [*Vertriebene*] coming from somewhere or other and others being driven away [*vertrieben*] somewhere else.' He had been like many others who had had to find their way home again at the end of the war: 'The way back was a long way for me, who, like millions coming back home from the war, owned not much more than except the hands in their pockets.'[110] He also expressed his gratitude to foreign authors who had helped him to find himself again.

It is doubtless because of this personal experience of being 'driven away' that Böll was not only sympathetic to but also directly helped Solzhenitsyn in his flight to the West.

At the end of his Banquet Speech, Böll recalled some other German laureates who had also suffered exile: Nelly Sachs, Thomas Mann ('driven away and expatriated') and Hermann Hesse, who had 'emigrated from his true self' and who 'had already long ceased to be a German citizen, when he was honoured here'.[111]

Finally he made the point that other exiled authors have made, that his only real and true home is the language in which he writes: '...my only valid pass, which no one needs to issue or extend for me, is the language, in which I write.'[112]

Böll views literature in a way which is compatible with Seifert's view of poetry as an effective medium of opposition. In his Nobel Lecture he says 'literature in its incarnation as a whole, in its message and shape, can clearly have a liberating effect...' Towards the end of this lecture he states also that it is meaningless to distinguish between committed and uncommitted literature. For him there is in literature an 'internationality of resistance'. Earlier in the lecture he had explained how this was possible because of the imperfections in all states: 'Countries, too, are always only approaching what they claim to be, and there can be no state which does not leave this gap between the verbal expression of its constitution and its realization, a space that remains, where poetry and resistance grow – and hopefully flourish. And there exists no form of literature which can succeed without this gap.' Literature also enables the world to perceive the universality of a particular and local grievance, what he calls 'the possibility of transference': 'it transfers us to South or North America, to Sweden, India, Africa. It can also transfer us to another class, another time, another religion and another race. It has – even in its bourgeois form – never been its goal to create strangeness, but to remove it.'[113]

But this universality of literature is paradoxically the reason why it cannot be judged and ranked: it can be perceived and understood only in relation to its cultural context. Thus protest may be a universal need, but the circumstances protested against are specific and localized. Böll does not state this explicitly, but when he says that it is not possible to judge literature to be successful or otherwise, this in effect undermines the Nobel ideal, or dream: '...there can be no successful literature, nor would there be any successful music or painting, because no one can already have seen the object it is striving to become, and in this respect everything that is superficially called modern, but which is better named living art, is experiment and discovery – and transient, can be estimated and measured only in its historical relativity, and it appears to me irrelevant to speak of eternal values, or to seek them.'[114]

While Gierow recognized Böll's life's work in his Presentation Speech, it is clear from his opening paragraph that it was Böll's most recent work *Group Portrait with Lady*, which tipped the scales in the writer's favour and convinced the committee that his time had come. And the theme which Gierow chose to emphasize was one akin to exile: homelessness. For Böll, asserts Gierow, homelessness meant not just 'those ill-fated individuals or human wreckage cast up outside the bulwarks of society'. For Böll the whole of his contemporary society was 'homeless': 'a society without a roof over its head, a derailed, displaced epoch...' In his conclusion, Gierow praises Böll for providing the kind of accessible literature in which such a 'homeless' society can feel at home. To define what he feels the author is seeking, he quotes Böll's own words to him in German, which translate as 'the search for a habitable language in a habitable land'.[115]

The Inner Exile

It should not be surprising that there was so much talk of exile from the fifties to the early seventies. So much of humanity, let alone writers, had been displaced, driven abroad, torn away from their traditional cultures and lifestyles in the preceding decades.

Salvatore Quasimodo (that's the Italian poet, not Hugo's hunchback immortalized by Charles Laughton) in his Nobel Lecture in 1959, 'The Poet and the Politician' (which is full of the broadest generalizations), reflects on why the poet has so often been driven into exile. He points out in his lecture the eternal tensions between the two types he is focusing on: 'While the poet is conscious of the politician's power, the politician notices the poet only when his voice reaches deep into the various social strata.' It has resulted, he argues, in the poet being exiled many times in the course of history. Whatever they may claim to the contrary, culture is the arch-enemy of the politician: 'In history the names of exiled poets are treated like human dice, while the politician claims to uphold culture but, in fact, tries only to reduce its power.' Modern media he sees not as the friend and disseminator of art but as the ally of the politician in fragmenting and therefore weakening the power of the artist: 'In our time the politician's defence against culture and thus against the poet operates both surreptitiously and openly in manifold ways. His easiest defence is the degradation of the concept of culture. Mechanical and scientific means, radio and television, help to break the unity of the arts, to favour a poetics that will not even disturb shadows.'[116] It would be interesting to speculate about the way in which Quasimodo would have reacted to the worldwide spread of the internet.

It should be noted that Quasimodo did not himself live in exile, except in so far as much of his poetry echoes his childhood and youth in Sicily, while he lived the rest of his life mostly in the northern part of Italy (Florence, Genoa and Milan mainly). He lived thus in a kind of 'inner exile', having also to keep his head down as a left-wing writer during the fascist period, and joining the Communist party only after the end of the war in 1946.

Prior to Quasimodo's Banquet Speech, a member of the Swedish Academy, E. Johnson, praised his work, addressing his words directly to the writer. They could just as easily have been directed to Böll in 1972 or Milosz in 1980: 'you understand the problems of our society, and your heart is compassionate toward the unfortunate, the disinherited'.[117]

Borders May Be Crossed

Some consideration has already been given to several other prominent exiles who won the Nobel Prize: Bunin and Brodsky, as well as Solzhenitsyn. And we have seen how exile was not only a reality for the Lithuanian-Polish writer Czesław Milosz but became a potent metaphor in his writing for the human condition in general. He allied himself thus, albeit probably unintentionally, with the ideals of Böll.

Milosz in fact spent the major part of his life in exile: although he spent the first forty years in Lithuania and Poland, he then spent some time in France and more than fifty years in the West in general. The majority of his works, both in poetry and prose, and mainly in Polish, were thus produced after he had emigrated to the USA in 1960. He became a United States citizen in 1970. He wasn't an American writer in any real sense however, always retaining his identity as a Polish-speaking poet from Lithuania. When the Eastern bloc collapsed he did spend some time in Poland again, but retained his home in the United States. He died in Kraków in 2004.

In his award ceremony speech Lars Gyllensten took Milosz's metaphor of exile as his recurrent theme. Exile is the human condition. He found in Milosz 'a passionate striving to make us intensely aware that we are living scattered abroad.' Man is alienated but seeking a home: 'Distance and presence characterize him in like degree. The same applies to his relationship to his new country, where he is a writer who must be translated to be understood.' At the end of his speech Gyllensten returns to his theme: 'You have often pictured human conditions as basically alienated – we are foreigners in this world and foreigners to one another.' But in his poetry Milosz made it possible for borders to be crossed, understanding and contact to take place: 'The Nobel Prize to you is also a token and a proof of the fact that borders may be crossed.'[118]

The Eternal Exile

Saint-John Perse (born as Alexis Leger) [1960] was another laureate who lived primarily in exile. He might be regarded as predestined for a life of exile. He was born in Guadeloupe in 1887, where his family had become established as landowners and lawyers for several generations. Due to developing anti-colonial feelings in Guadeloupe, the Leger family decided it would be wise to return to France, but it seems that Saint-John felt himself to be an expatriate there. After his studies he joined the French diplomatic service, which led to him spending most of his time in yet other countries, first Spain, Germany and the United Kingdom. Then from 1916 to 1921 he was sent to the French embassy in what was then called Peking (Beijing). From 1932 he served as General Secretary of the French Foreign Office until 1940, accompanying the French Foreign Minister to the Munich Conference in 1938. After the fall of France in May 1940, he was dismissed from his post because of his anti-Nazi sentiments, and in mid-July of that year he went into exile in the United States. With the help of the poet Archibald MacLeish he acquired a post at the Library of Congress, where he stayed till 1947. One of the first long poems he wrote in America bore the title 'Exile'. Though given a home at Giens in Provence, he still spent most of his time in the United States till he died in 1975.

In his Banquet Speech Perse explored the relationships between poetry and science, claiming for poetry a central role in all human endeavours: 'refusing to divorce art from life, love from perception, it is action, it is passion, it is power, and always the innovation which extends borders. Love is its hearth-fire, insurrection its law, its place is everywhere, in anticipation.' In an at times florid prose style he celebrated poetry for the perspicuity of its insights: 'The obscurity for which it is reproached pertains not to its own nature, which is to illuminate, but to the night which it explores, the night of the soul and the mystery in which human existence is shrouded. Obscurity is banished from its expression and this expression is no less exacting than that of science.'[119]

The Odyssey of a Diplomat

Another poet, diplomat and exile to win the Nobel Prize was Giorgos Seferis [1963]. He was born near Smyrna (present-day Izmir, Turkey), and undertook part of his secondary education in Athens. He then studied law at the Sorbonne in Paris from 1918 to 1925. Because of the political situation in the region he was not able to visit his birthplace again until 1950. In 1926 he joined the Royal Greek Ministry of Foreign Affairs and thereby began a long career as a diplomat: which included postings in Great Britain and then in Albania. During the Second World War he went with the Free Greek Government to Crete, Egypt, South Africa and Italy. After the war came further diplomatic postings: Turkey, Great Britain, Lebanon, Jordan, Iraq and Syria.

Anders Österling, in his award ceremony speech, stressed that theme that was to be taken up again in 1972 by Böll: 'homelessness – ever the fate of an oppressed and scattered people – was to play a decisive role during his adult years in more ways than one.'[120] And in his Banquet Speech Seferis made a plea for everyone 'to listen to that human voice which we call poetry', and which we so easily neglect: 'Threatened, it has always found a refuge; denied, it has always instinctively taken root again in unexpected places. It recognizes no small nor large parts of the world; its place is in the hearts of men the world over. It has the charm of escaping from the vicious circle of custom.'[121]

Seferis's Nobel Lecture focused on significant and influential poets during the history of Greek culture ('Some Notes on Modern Greek Tradition'). What he admired in the work of the Greek poet who lived in Alexandria, Constantine Cavafy, was clearly an aspect of himself: 'he loved countries and periods in which frontiers are not well defined, in which personalities and beliefs are fluid. Many of his characters are partly pagan and partly Christian, or live in a mixed environment.'[122]

Born in Jerusalem

1966 was one of the few years when the Nobel Prize was awarded to two laureates: Shmuel Agnon and Nelly Sachs. Agnon wrote in Hebrew and delivered his Banquet Speech in that language. It is imbued throughout with a sense of his intense religious dedication: '...the good God put it into the hearts of the sages of the illustrious Academy to bestow that great and esteemed prize upon an author who writes in the sacred tongue...'[123] He was an exile in another special sense, being part of that diaspora which spread Jewish families around the world. He was born in Buczacz, in Eastern Galicia (now Buchach, in the Ukraine). He spoke Yiddish with his family, learned Hebrew from an early age and was introduced to German literature by his mother. In 1907 he went to Palestine, and in 1913 moved to Germany, staying in Berlin and Bad Homburg. In 1924 he moved back with his wife and child to Palestine, where he spent the rest of his life.

In his Banquet Speech he revealed that while he felt he shared the fate of many Jews to be a nation in exile, he also felt that his spiritual home was in Israel: 'As a result of the historic catastrophe in which Titus of Rome destroyed Jerusalem and Israel was exiled from its land, I was born in one of the cities of the Exile. But always I regarded myself as one who was born in Jerusalem.'[124]

The Messenger from Latin America

The work of Miguel Ángel Asturias [1967], like that of other exiles already considered, was nevertheless rooted in the culture and traditions of his native Guatemala. The prime focus of his writing is the myths and beliefs of the indigenous peoples of his home country. One major work, and one of his most well-known, *The President*, is a denunciation of dictatorship.

A brief summary of his life reveals the extent of his time in exile. He was born (1899) and raised in Guatemala, but in 1923, after receiving a degree in law, he went to Paris, where he studied anthropology and ethnology at the Sorbonne. He returned to Guatemala in 1933 and worked as a journalist before becoming a diplomat. From 1946 onwards he served as a diplomat in various Central and South American countries (Mexico, Argentina and El Salvador) and was posted to Paris in 1952. Asturias supported the government of Jacobo Árbenz, but when it fell, he was sent into exile and stripped of his citizenship. At first he lived in Buenos Aires and Chile. But in 1966, with the return of democracy to Guatemala, he was given back his citizenship and appointed ambassador to France, serving there till 1970. He spent his final years in Madrid, where he died in 1974, and was buried in the Père Lachaise Cemetery in Paris.

It is clear from the award ceremony speech made by Anders Österling, that Asturias was regarded by the committee not only as a brilliant and original writer but also as a representative of South American culture in general: 'Latin America today can boast an active group of prominent writers, a multivoiced chorus in which individual contributions are not readily discernible. Asturias's work is nevertheless vast, bold, and outstanding enough to arouse interest outside of his own literary milieu.' And in conclusion, addressing Asturias as 'Mr Ambassador' (the post he held in Paris at the time) Österling said 'We take pleasure in welcoming you as a messenger from Latin America, its people, its spirit, and its future.'[125]

The award of the prize to Asturias was perceived by many as recognition of the growing importance of the Latin American novel. Leading international newspapers certainly took this line.

It is interesting also to note that Asturias was in competition that year with two well-respected Europeans. Gierow had advised that the main contest ought to be between Asturias, W.H. Auden and Graham Greene. It seems that Greene had both determined supporters and opponents in the Academy at that time. But it was generally agreed that Greene's most significant work lay in the past. At that time the committee preferred to give consideration to work which had been insufficiently regarded.

Asturias himself, in his Banquet Speech, certainly regarded the prize as being given to him as an individual who nevertheless represented South American culture as a whole: '...our novels appear to Europeans as illogical or aberrant. They are not shocking for the sake of shock effects. It is just that what happened to us was shocking. Continents submerged in the sea, races castrated as they surged to independence, and the fragmentation of the New World. As the antecedents of a literature these are already tragic.' And a little later he adds: 'We are peoples from worlds which have nothing like the orderly unfolding of European conflicts, always human in their dimensions. The dimensions of our conflicts in the past centuries have been catastrophic.'[126]

And it as an identifiable phenomenon with shared characteristics that he described the history of the South American novel in his Nobel Lecture, to which he gave the title 'The Latin American Novel, testimony of an Epoch'. He clearly also saw the writer in exile as playing an important and significant role in the literature of South America, In the lecture he focuses on five writers, not so well-known in the rest of the world, who 'gave birth to a literature of exiles, which is – and will continue to be – a testimony of its epoch'.[127]

This account by no means exhausts the number of Nobel Prize laureates who have spent much of their productive life in exile.

There have been Elias Canetti [1981], Gao Xingjian [2000], Herta Müller [2009], and many others who spent large parts of their lives living and working in countries other than those in which they were born or for which they held citizenship. Many of these are considered in other contexts.

The Nobel Complex

The Chequered Life of a Chinese Writer

One particular award merits an in-depth case study. It illustrates various anomalies in the Nobel Prize awards process and raises questions about whether it can ever be entirely free from political considerations.

In 2000, Gao Xingjian was the first Chinese writer to win the Nobel Prize in Literature: he was also living in exile as a French citizen at the time. Many other Chinese writers and intellectuals found themselves on an unsteady footing with regard to their reaction. There were those who celebrated the event wholeheartedly and those who rejected it outright. The problem was that the Chinese had been suffering for many years from a collective psychological disturbance, what has been dubbed the 'Nobel Complex': an obsessive concern that one's country should win a Nobel Prize. This malaise had spread especially extensively on the mainland. Chinese culture had not been the only one to be afflicted with this condition: it spread also to Japan and Korea.

While Gao Xingjian may have won over critics, theorists and members of the Nobel Committee in the West, he has not done his best to win friends and influence people in his homeland.

As a child, in the 1940s, and under his mother's influence, in Jiangxi Province, China, Gao developed enthusiasms for writing, painting and the theatre. He also read a great deal of Western literature. In 1950 the family moved to Nanjing and in 1957 he attended Beijing Foreign Studies University. He graduated in French in 1962 and became a professional translator. After some time spent in the countryside during the Cultural Revolution, he returned to Beijing in 1975 and worked as a French translator for a magazine. As a member of the Committee of Foreign Relations of the Chinese Association of Writers he visited Paris in 1979. In 1980 he became a playwright and screenplay writer with the Beijing People's Art Theatre. As a result of being misdiagnosed with lung cancer in 1986 he undertook a ten-month journey along the Yangtze River, from which emerged his novel *Soul Mountain* (published in Taiwan in 1989). In an interview with Maya Jaggi (*The Guardian*, Saturday, 2nd August 2008) Gao stated that he believed that it was his reaction to the events in Tiananmen Square in 1989 that made it inevitable that he would have to go into exile. He condemned the massacre openly on French television and resigned from the Communist Party, which he had joined in 1962. He then applied for political asylum in France after tearing up his Chinese passport. He officially became a French citizen in 1997.

The explicit reasons for awarding him the Nobel Prize were given by Prof. Göran Malmqvist in his award ceremony speech. Gao 'made very important contributions to the theoretical debate concerning the structure and functions of drama and the novel in China during the eighties'. And his novel *Soul Mountain* 'stands out as one of the foremost works in twentieth-century Chinese literature.' Malmqvist also cites his 'vivid sense of alienation in a politics-ridden society' and stresses that his critique is not one-sided: 'he also castigates strict Confucian orthodoxy as well as Marxist ideology and their respective demands for obedience and uniformity'. In conclusion Malmqvist reassures Gao that while he may be living in exile, the Chinese language is his true home: 'You did not leave China empty-handed. You have come to look on the native language which you brought with you when you left China as your true and real country.'[128] Many of Malmqvist's arguments found little sympathy however with most writers and intellectuals in the Chinese-speaking world, especially back in the land of Gao's birth.

Near the start of his extensive lecture Gao says that he does 'not want to waste this talk on literature by saying too much about politics and history', but he cannot avoid it to a large extent, especially as he is concerned to separate literature from politics: 'Once literature is contrived as the hymn of the nation, the flag of the race, the mouthpiece of a political party or the voice of a class or group, it can be employed as a mighty and all-engulfing tool of propaganda.'[129]

Thus in effect he devotes considerable time to reflections on the relationship between literature and politics. Clearly the Cultural Revolution scarred him and was the primary cause (if Tiananmen Square was the last straw) of his eventually going into exile: 'The writer who sought to avoid suicide or being silenced and furthermore to express his own voice had no option but to go into exile.' It was during the period of the Cultural Revolution in fact that he learned the value of talking to oneself: '…to write even in secret was to risk one's life. To maintain one's intellectual autonomy one could only talk to oneself, and it had to be in utmost secrecy.' It helped him however to understand what was fundamental to literature: 'It can be said that talking to oneself is the starting point of literature and that using language to communicate is secondary.' It is this latter principle which has made him especially problematic to many of his fellow countrymen. For Gao literature has 'no duty to the masses'. He admires a literature which is pure self-expression and does not 'warm' to its readers: 'Cold literature is a literature that will flee in order to survive.'[130] And so he did.

If this concept of literature sounds too negative, he explained it more clearly in his interview with *The Guardian*. As paraphrased by Maya Jaggi 'cold literature' means living without ideologies, without 'isms', detached from 'consumerist pressures' as well as 'political agendas'.[131] Literature should essentially bear witness to events in the world.

One academic, who has studied the Chinese preoccupation with the Nobel Prize, its Nobel Complex, and the reactions to Gao's award in depth, is Julia Lovell, in her book *The Politics of Cultural Capital: China's Quest for a Nobel Prize in Literature*, 2006. The book has the depth, breadth and extensive justification for every point that one expects of a doctoral thesis. A pertinent intellectual history (*Geistesgeschichte*) of culture East and West going back several centuries is provided. Her final chapter and the last part of the penultimate chapter are the most closely related to the concerns of the present book, and I am indebted to her research in what follows.

When news of the award reached China, the public had to wait thirty-six hours before the state press, *Renmin ribao*, announced it, claiming that the Nobel Committee had used political criteria in its choice: 'this shows that the Nobel Prize for Literature has essentially been used for political purposes and thus lost its authority'.[132] Lovell also researched the internet responses to the news. Reactions ranged from joy, to puzzlement and resentment. The instinctual first response, before learning about the full circumstances, was delight that a Chinese writer had won. But Lovell points out: 'very few people in Mainland China had read the works for which Gao was awarded the prize when the Nobel announcement was made.'[133] There was general criticism of the view expressed by the Chinese Writers' Association that the Swedish Academy had acted politically. The irony was that it was known that the Chinese Writers' Association itself always acted politically. But there have been many rapid changes in China in recent years, and many Mainland Chinese feel that Gao writes and talks about a China that no longer exists. There is now greater, if imperfect, freedom of expression. Lovell writes: 'According to many critics and writers, Chinese authors could now write about anything they wanted without fear of severe reprisal, and even with the prospect of financial gain – only as long as they did not write about politics.'[134] The limits to this freedom are demonstrated by the protective measures which Lovell herself felt obliged to adopt for her interviews: in order to gain true opinions she had to guarantee anonymity so that, apart from a few well-known figures, her sources are identified as Poet A, Critic C, etc.

The resentment felt against Gao's award concerns mainly the fact that he has somehow, as a result of the prize, become regarded as a representative of China: 'There is a feeling among contemporary Chinese writers that China has changed greatly since 1989 and that exiles, seized upon by the west as representatives, are not necessarily qualified spokesmen.'[135] Lovell quotes Poet A who expresses the point in a vivid simile: 'I think that giving Gao this prize is like giving a ping pong player a golf prize. Tell me, is this really a prize for Chinese literature? Or is it a prize for the political things that westerners like to read about China?'[136]

The case of Gao Xingjian has also brought up for consideration the role of the 'Nobel Complex' in other countries. The complex can be loosely defined as an obsessive concern to gain international recognition for the cultural and scientific accomplishments of a country. In relation specifically to recognition for the national literature, there has also been evidence, apart from in China, of the spread of the complex in Japan, as Lovell has testified: 'The Japanese government made strenuous efforts in translation and promotion to bring Kawabata and other Japanese authors to international and Nobel attention in the 1960s, in the lead up to the awarding of the 1967 Nobel Prize to Kawabata.'[137] It is not so well known that the complex is also virulent in South Korea.

Go West Young Eun

For several years, some say for at least a decade, academics, critics and journalists in South Korea have made up their minds that one Korean writer above all others has earned the right to be awarded the Nobel Prize in Literature. One cannot of course know any details of proposals and of the deliberations of the committee over recent years, but in South Korea it is generally accepted that campaigns on his behalf have been energetically pursued. The writer's name is Ko Un, as written according to an older transcription system. This is the spelling he seems to prefer, and it is the one adopted by most journalists and other writers, although according to the transcription system currently in use for the Korean language it should be 'Go Eun'.

Ko would certainly seem to have a lot going for him in terms of his general achievements and commitments, but it has to be honestly said that, given the requirement that a laureate be alive at the time of the award, time might be running out for a man who will become an octogenarian in 2013.

Born Ko Untae he was at school in North Jeolla Province when the Korean War broke out in 1950. He suffered emotionally and physically during this time, witnessing massacres by both right-wing and left-wing groups. As a teenager he attempted suicide several times. He became a Buddhist monk in 1952, one year before the end of the war in 1953, and started writing poetry during that period. He returned to a secular life in 1962, but Buddhism continues to influence his writing. In the 1970s Ko became involved in various social issues and the democracy movement. For his political activities he was sent to prison four times (1974, 1979, 1980 and 1989) under various dictatorial regimes. He is mainly known for his large output of poetry, but he has also published works of fiction, autobiography, drama, essays, travel books and translations from classical Chinese. His works amount to about 135 volumes.

In recent years it has become common in South Korea, when the name of the Nobel laureate has been announced, for there to be general lament and complaint in the media that Ko Un has been overlooked yet again. An article in *The Korea Herald*, 8th October 2010, bore the headline 'Poet Ko Un misses out on

Nobel again.' Its writer, Kim Yoon-mi, claimed to have close contact with the Swedish media: 'Literature experts in the media in Stockholm had bet on Ko winning earlier.' An article by Moon So-young and Lee Sun-min in the *Korea Joongang Daily*, 9th October 2010, bears as its opening line: 'The Korean literary world's long-cherished desire to have a Nobel laureate was dashed again this week.' And in *The Korea Herald* again on 10th October, there was a citation from Associated Press that a literature expert for the Swedish newspaper *Dagens Nyheter*, Maria Schottenius, had expected it to be either Ko or the Syrian poet Adonis that year. In 2011, according to an article in the *Los Angeles Times*, 29th September 2011, Ko Un was still quite high in the betting list for that year (according to Ladbrokes he was 6th with odds at 14/1). One cannot help but wonder if it had something to do with the exceptionally large Korean community in Los Angeles. The same Korean journalists lamenting Ko's dashed chances also brought out the familiar accusations against the Nobel Committee: the *Korea Joongang Daily*, 9th October 2010, claimed that 'the award has gone to other writers, mostly European novelists'. And in *The Korea Herald*, 10th October 2010, one can read: 'The awardees in recent years are mostly European and the genre is also limited to novels, while poets are relatively sidelined in the prestigious awards.' And Song Won-seop wrote in the *Korea Joongang Daily*, 11th October 2010, that 'writers who stood out against dictatorship won the favour of the judges', so for that reason it had been hoped that the committee would have looked with favour on Ko Un. But this assumes a basic political bias of the committee, which, as we have seen, is, on Espmark's evidence, debatable. It is interesting to note that in general critics of the prize in South Korea were not so vociferous in 2011, when the prize was awarded to an another elderly poet (Tomas Tranströmer).

Ko has at least already got his foot in the door of Scandinavian awards, winning the Norwegian Bjørnson Order for Literature prize in 2005, named after the winner of the Nobel Prize in Literature in 1903, and the Cikada Prize, a Swedish literary prize for East Asian Poets, in 2008. While he lives the nation hopes. The Nobel Complex depends for its survival, like the existence of the Greek gods, on humanity's belief in its necessity. It is also much like political campaigning: it is difficult to prove that it is effective, but no one dares to give it up. As long as various countries and institutions within those countries believe they can influence the decisions of the Swedish Academy, they will continue to attempt to do so.

Provincialism and its Limitations, or Small Can Be Beautiful

The Nobel Complex has its roots in nationalism, and nationalism is akin to provincialism: it is just that one concerns a larger area than the other. And is there really so much difference between a small region and a small country? Provincialism (concern for very localized issues and lifestyle) is not necessarily a bad thing, and can be celebrated in ways which bring out the universality of the particular. It can have the charm of the unique and the quaintness of the backwater, but it also has its limitations in appealing to global audiences. It is an issue that several of the Nobel Prizewinners have taken up and even exemplified.

Revitalising the Roots

William Butler Yeats' Banquet Speech, on receiving his award in 1923, focused particularly on the concept of provincialism. It is clear that for him provincialism meant too warm a preoccupation with one's own corner of the world, a kind of cultural inward-looking: 'Thirty years ago a number of Irish writers met together in societies and began a remorseless criticism of the literature of their country. It was their dream that by freeing it from provincialism they might win for it European recognition.'[138] He knew that his receiving of the Nobel Prize would be regarded by those writers as a fulfilment of that dream.

In his Nobel Lecture on 'The Irish Dramatic Movement' he explained that it was this reaction against provincialism that drove him to encourage literature in English rather than Gaelic. He had helped to found societies in which 'clerks, working men, men of all classes, could study those Irish poets, novelists, and historians who had written in English, and as much of Gaelic literature as had been translated into English.'[139] And it was also the reason why, in order to reach a wider public, he helped to found an English language theatre.

It is clear however that Yeats was not encouraging writers to turn their backs on the cultures of small isolated communities. Rather he wanted to bring out their virtues in contrast to the negative aspects of modern life. In this spirit he encouraged the young writer John Synge: 'I did not, however, see what was to come when I advised John Synge to go to a wild island off the Galway coast and study its life because that life "had never been expressed in literature"…When he found that wild island he became happy for the first time, escaping as he said "from the nullity of the rich and the squalor of the poor".'[140] The general aim was thus to provide access for modern man to his cultural roots. Of the plays that he, Synge and Lady Gregory were producing at the time Yeats said: 'They bring the imagination and speech of the country, all that political tradition descended from the Middle Ages, to the people of the town.'[141]

The Nobel Prize website includes some additions that Yeats made to his lecture when it was published in *The Bounty of Sweden*. In one of these additions he linked his concerns about provincial Irish literature with broader issues of political freedom and freedom of expression: 'The danger to art and literature comes today from the tyranny and persuasions of revolutionary societies and forms of political and religious propaganda.' He also quoted the writer Josef Strzygowski, who believed that those who are not willing to accept the fact that art must be subordinated to politics have only two options: to distance themselves from the issues, either mentally or by cultural exile. In

Strzygowski's words quoted by Yeats they 'must either emigrate or remain aloof'.[142]

Transformations of a Den-life

Seventy-two years later another Irish poet who won the award expressed related sentiments. In his Nobel lecture, 'Crediting Poetry', Seamus Heaney [1995] wrote: 'In the nineteen forties, when I was the eldest child of an ever-growing family in rural Co. Derry, we crowded together in the three rooms of a traditional thatched farmstead and lived a kind of den-life which was more or less emotionally and intellectually proofed against the outside world.' Later he emphasized that the experience of being born and brought up in Northern Ireland had stayed with him, even though he has lived in a kind of exile from it, 'having lived with that place even though I have lived out of it for the past quarter of a century'.[143]

Heaney devoted a considerable part of his lecture to what Yeats had said in his, and he noted that his predecessor had stressed how the provincial, the local, could be employed to bring about change: 'He came to Sweden to tell the world that the local work of poets and dramatists had been as important to the transformation of his native place and times as the ambushes of guerrilla armies...'[144]

Far from the Mighty of the Earth

In 1955 the award went to Halldór Laxness, who was, in his own words (in his Banquet Speech) 'a writer from one of the most remote islands in the world'. He was influenced most as a writer not by other writers but by the people he grew up with in his native Iceland: '...they have formed and influenced me and, to this day, their effect on me is greater than that of any of the world's great masters or pioneers could possibly have been.' What knowledge of literary traditions he acquired came to him through his family: 'My father and mother, but above all, my grandmother, who taught me hundreds of lines of old Icelandic poetry before I ever learned the alphabet.' Later he added: 'I spent my entire childhood in an environment in which the mighty of the earth had no place outside story books and dreams.' He felt himself lucky to have been born within 'that community of one hundred and fifty thousand men and women who form the book-loving nation that we Icelanders are.' He felt it to be his good fortune indeed 'to be born into a nation so steeped in centuries of poetry and literary tradition'.[145]

While he was thankful for the prize and the 'measure of material well-being brought about by money', he was also very much aware that he should not forget his origins, 'as a man of the people' nor should he 'ever lose his sense of belonging with the humble of the earth'.[146]

There had been some concerns in the Nobel Committee discussions about Laxness' political views. Espmark explains how when the choice of Laxness was announced, some American andFrench commentators saw a connection, because of the author's known communist sympathies, with the broader political situation in Europe at that time: there were signs of a détente between the West and the Soviet Union.[147] An article in the French magazine L'Express revealed some satisfaction that the prize appeared to have been compromised by the fact that it was clearly a political gesture 'in favour of a local mediocrity'. In L'Humanité there was praise of the choice as a celebration of the communist cause.[148] But in a radio interview on 27th October, Österling revealed some of the committee's actual thinking on the matter. They were more worried about his artistic integrity: '…there had been reservations on the ground that the author's ever-present social and political involvement was at times so strong that it threatened the artistic qualities of his work.'[149]

Espmark points out that contrary to the views expressed in the press there was rather evidence of the persistence of anti-Marxist views on the committee. He quotes the committee's view that 'Marxist convictions, however honest they may be, lead in many instances to anachronistic views that disturb and damage his perspective on reality.'[150]

Magnificent Insignificance

There are clear parallels between the life and work of the Icelander Halldór Laxness and that of the Finnish novelist Frans Eemil Sillenpää [1939]. This becomes clear in the Presentation Speech and the account, also described confusingly as a 'presentation' on the website, of the writer and his work on the occasion of Sillenpää's award, both delivered by Per Hallström, the Permanent Secretary at the time. Hallström spoke in the Presentation Speech of the obvious pleasure taken 'in rendering the everyday life of the peasants, strongly attached to the earth from which it draws its strength'.[151] In the so-called presentation Hallström describes more closely the motifs of Sillenpää's novels and novellas, 'which are almost exclusively about his native land (a small region of Finnish peasants) from the scanty, limited circumstances in which he grew up'.[152] And (in the Presentation Speech) he quoted the author's words back at him, concerning his best known work, *The Maid Silja*: 'everything that touches Silja is generally of a magnificent insignificance'.[153]

If Finland is a small country with problems and issues which do not generally register with the rest of the world, it has nevertheless had its conflicts which were microcosms of global conflicts. The novel which made Sillenpää's fame (*Meek Heritage*, 1919) dealt with the effects on the country and its people of the civil war between nationalists and communists. In his narrative he avoided analysis of the heroic fight for liberation from Russian domination, and focused instead on the social struggles of his people, showing how the poor peasants depended entirely on the good will of their despotic landlords.

The choice of Sillenpää for the prize provided another occasion for debate about the presumed political aspects of the prize. Espmark is unequivocal: 'From a political point of view the most questioned prize of the first few decades was the one given in the autumn of 1939 to Frans Eemil Sillenpää.'[154] In his account Anders Österling pointed out that it should not seem surprising if the Academy's decision was influenced by Finland's contemporary struggle against the superior power of the Soviet Union. But Espmark stresses that the author had been under consideration as a nominee since 1930, and that Hallström had already submitted seven consecutive specialist reports on him. In 1939 the competition was between the Dutch writer Johan Huizinga, Hermann Hesse, Sillenpää and the Flemish novelist Stijn Streuvels. Espmark provides a detailed account of how the balance in the voting changed. It is noticeable that, if anything, the situation in Finland was in danger of having a negative effect on the committee's decision: 'In this first round – just at the time when news was coming in of the threat to Finland – a majority of seven out of the twelve present wanted to withhold the prize.' Espmark's conclusion about the final choice would seem to be fair: 'The outcome was primarily a result of election arithmetic that was dictated by hesitation about Hesse. No reference to the Soviet threat is visible as a motive, either in the minutes or in the letters.'[155] Of course the political situation may have influenced individual members in their reflections. It seems likely however that the final decision was made to demonstrate that the political situation was *not* a determining factor. As with Laxness later therefore the committee had endeavoured in the case of Sillenpää to avert the effect of political bias, and to resist succumbing to it.

The Limits of the Local

To conclude these reflections on provincialism a few words should be allowed to T.S. Eliot [1948], who, in his Banquet Speech, drew attention to the limits of provincialism, especially in relation to poetry. What he calls 'the local' clearly incorporates within it the concept of provincialism: 'Poetry is usually considered the most local of all the arts. Painting, sculpture, architecture, music, can be enjoyed by all who see or hear. But language, especially the language of poetry, is a different matter. Poetry, it might seem, separates people instead of uniting them.' But 'while language constitutes a barrier, poetry itself gives us a reason for trying to overcome the barrier'. And in making a deliberate effort to overcome the barrier we gain an understanding of another people, 'an understanding we can get in no other way'. Every poet must also owe much to poets in other languages, not least for their recreations of his or her poetry in their own tongues. Translation '…must be also a kind of recreation of his poems by other poets…' Thus, on the one hand, Eliot grants the limitations of the local aspects of poetry: 'in the work of every poet there will certainly be much that can only appeal to those who inhabit the same region, or speak the same language, as the poet.' But on the other, he wishes to assert 'the supra-national value of poetry'.[156]

The Historians

While many laureates have shown themselves to be concerned about, and even obsessed with, the history of their countries, there have been few actual historians who have won the prize (a point for would-be laureates to note when sizing up the opposition). There have been only two in fact: Theodor Mommsen [1902] and Winston Churchill [1953]. The dearth is due to the fact that, though the statutes permit consideration of non-literary writers for the prize, the committee itself has come over the years to prefer the choice of purely literary figures.

Apologist for Enlightened Despotism

C.D. af Wirsén justified the committee's choice of the historian Theodor Mommsen in the second year of the prize, 1902, by quoting Nobel's will and adding a lengthy gloss of his own in the Presentation Speech. He was also clearly opening the way for other kinds of writers than purely literary ones in the future when he said: 'the second paragraph of the Nobel statutes states that "Literature" should include not only belles-lettres, "but also other writings that in form or content show literary value". This definition sanctions the award of the Nobel Prize in Literature to philosophers, writers on religious subjects, scientists, and historians, provided that their work is distinguished by artistic excellence of presentation as well as by the high value of its content.'[157]

Mommsen is thus praised for the monumental nature of his achievement and his style. Wirsén cites Mommsen's contribution as editor to all fifteen volumes of the *Corpus Inscriptionum Latinarum* (started in 1867 but not finished until 1959), and for his original research 'in Roman law, epigraphy, numismatics, the chronology of Roman history, and general Roman history'.[158] He is praised also for being an expert on agriculture in Carthage. The prize was awarded primarily however for the monumental work for which he is most known by the educated public: his *History of Rome* (1854–55, 1885). In Wirsén's analysis of this work he reveals clearly his sympathies for the conservative values revealed in the work, its essential apology for enlightened despotism: '...it must be emphasized that Mommsen never glorifies brute power, but extols that power which serves the high goals of the state.' Wirsén also shows sympathy for Mommsen's presenting the family as the model for a state: 'Concerning G. Gracchus, the inspired revolutionary whose measures he sometimes praises and sometimes blames, he says that every state is built on sand unless the ruler and the governed are tied together by a common morality. A healthy family life is to him the core of the nation.' Wirsén argued that Mommsen's description of the Roman people reflects these values clearly. Mommsen showed 'how the Roman's obedience to the state was linked to the obedience of son to father', 'how the Senate took care of public affairs in an honourable manner', 'how caesarism became a necessity', 'and how absolutism in many cases would have caused less hardship than the oligarchic rule'.[159]

Espmark has little to say about the choice of Mommsen, except that it proved to be an exception and that most commentators on the choice have expressed concern about the fact that he was not a literary figure: 'Reservations about Mommsen... have been mainly due to the fact that his brilliant achievement falls outside the field of literature.'[160]

A Caesar with the Pen of Cicero

While honoured for his writing as an historian, Churchill was of course also a politician, and a major historical figure. It has been noted previously that other laureates have held government appointments, but being a major leader of the western world in the fight against Fascism in the Second World War does rather set Churchill apart.

When Dag Hammarskjöld first became a member of the Nobel Committee in 1955 he expressed some unease about possible political aspects of several of the committee's judgements. In a letter to Sten Selander (12th May 1955) he wrote: 'Churchill-Hemingway-Sholokhov: is the Swedish Academy a literary committee in the Foreign Office?'[161]

Churchill had been a candidate since immediately after the war in 1946. Espmark reports that various objections were made in the Academy's deliberations. It was felt that it would be too obviously an award to 'the winner of World War II'. The postponement to 1953 indicated that the committee then 'felt that a sufficient distance from his wartime exploits had been gained'. Nils Ahlund, an Academy member who was also an historian, felt that it was mainly for his oratory that Churchill deserved the prize.[162]

Churchill's position was further complicated by the fact that in 1953 he was also a prime minister and 'leader of one of the key powers in the cold war world'.[163] But eventually, in the award ceremony speech by S. Siwertz, the emphasis was put primarily on Churchill's qualities as a writer: 'very seldom have great statesmen and warriors also been great writers. One thinks of Julius Caesar, Marcus Aurelius, and even Napoleon, whose letters to Josephine during the first Italian campaign certainly have passion and splendor. But the man who can most readily be compared with Sir Winston Churchill is Disraeli.' Later Siwertz 'is tempted to resort to portray him as a Caesar who also has the gift of

Cicero's pen'. Apart from Churchill's accounts of battles, Siwertz also praises his early writing: 'it is the exciting and colourful side of Churchill's writing which perhaps first strikes the reader. Besides much else, *My Early Life* (1930) is also one of the world's most entertaining adventure stories.' His accomplishments as a biographer (of the Duke of Marlborough as well as of himself) are praised for revealing his ability at 'character-drawing'. But in conclusion Siwertz supports Ahlund's assessment: 'With his great speeches he has, perhaps, himself erected his most enduring monument.'[164]

The committee seem also to have been very much aware that in awarding the prize to Churchill they were also very much legitimizing the status of the prize itself, having greatness thrust upon it, as it were. To Lady Churchill, who received the award on her husband's behalf, Siwertz said at the end of his speech 'A literary prize is intended to cast luster over the author, but here it is the author who gives luster to the prize.'[165]

Only a brief mention is made elsewhere on the Nobel website (in their brief biography) of another book of Churchill's which became very popular: *Painting as a Pastime* (1948).

In the Banquet Speech read by Lady Churchill, Churchill recognized that the Swedish Academy was 'accepted as impartial, authoritative, and sincere throughout the civilized world,' but added, with his characteristic wry humour, 'I do hope you are right.'[166]

The Philosophers

Other writers may have dabbled in philosophical thought from time to time, but there were only three actual professional philosophers who were awarded the Nobel Prize in Literature: Rudolf Eucken [1908], Henri Bergson [1927] and Bertrand Russell [1950]. As no other philosopher has been awarded the prize in more than half a century, it would be unwise to raise your hopes of winning it, if you happen to be reading this when you should be marking undergraduate papers on epistemology. You would need to dabble a bit more in literature on the side to stand a chance. Russell did just that. However his collections of stories, *Satan in the Suburbs and Other Stories* (1953) and *Nightmares of Eminent Persons and Other Stories* (1954), were not published until after the award: perhaps he felt he had to justify it somehow. The three philosophers in question, Eucken, Bergson and Russell are as different as chalk and cheese, or perhaps it would be more appropriate to say as chalk, syrup and cheese, respectively.

The Pale Idealist

Starting with the chalk. Rudolf Christoph Eucken was born in Lower Saxony, Germany. He studied at Göttingen and Berlin universities. His Ph.D. at Göttingen was in classical philology and ancient history, but he discovered that he had a bent for the philosophical aspects of theology. After working as a school-teacher for five years, he was appointed Professor of Philosophy at the University of Basel in Switzerland. In 1874 he took up a similar post at the University of Jena in Germany. From 1913–14 he was a guest lecturer at New York University. He stayed in Jena until he retired in 1920.

Harald Hjärne, in his Presentation Speech, described him as 'one of the most prominent thinkers of our age'.[167] Of his age he certainly was, for few speak of him nowadays. The official citation stated that the award was made 'in recognition of his earnest search for truth, his penetrating power of thought, his wide range of vision, and the warmth and strength of presentation with which in his numerous works he has vindicated and developed an idealistic philosophy'.[168] But the 'warmth and strength of presentation' seems to have been lacking somewhat in his Nobel Lecture, or it is does not come across in the printed text.

According to Espmark, Eucken was in any case the winner by default.[169] There was apparently a heated discussion that year about whether to choose Selma Lagerlöf, the Swedish writer, or the Englishman Algernon Swinburne. The dilemma was eventually solved by giving it to neither and awarding it instead to Eucken. It is hard at this distance in time to imagine how someone Espmark described as 'the pale Jena philosopher' ever came up for consideration. In the official report he was described as 'an original but hardly epoch-making thinker'. While his diction was praised, it was also lamented that his writing did not have the beauty 'of a Plato, a Kant, or a Schelling'. It appears that Wirsén could not agree with the final choice and refused to give the award ceremony speech, passing the buck instead to Hjärne. Hjärne was one of the few members of the Academy with a more positive view of Eucken. In a letter to Wirsén of 13th October 1908, he wrote that it would be good for the committee to show 'that we were not afraid to select a worthy recipient on our own account, without feeling we ought to wait until we can come with our diploma and our pennies simply to crown a world reputation already safely established'.[170] This does however indirectly confirm that Eucken was not generally rated very highly in the Academy.

From Hjärne's speech it also seems that the 'lofty and sound idealism' which clearly dominated the committee's thinking in that first decade of the prize may well have particularly influenced their final choice in 1908. He talked of the 'confident and rising idealism today in the intellectual life not only of Germany but everywhere on the higher and freer levels of civilized life...' And later he allied the laureate with the great classical philosophers: '...no branch of philosophy has produced so many marked profiles as realistic idealism. Socrates and Plato were led by this idealism to hold that philosophy is a search for truth rather than a fixed dogma...' In his reply Eucken acknowledged this tribute and spoke with enthusiasm of the idealism for which he had always striven.[171]

Eucken's very long Nobel lecture, entitled 'Naturalism or Idealism', reinforces his philosophical preferences. Naturalism for him was a philosophical standpoint which reduced human life to the utilitarian purpose of its own preservation, 'Idealism, on the other hand, maintains the emancipation of inwardness; according to it the disparate phenomena of life coalesce in an all-embracing inner world. At the same time, idealism demands that human life should be governed by its peculiar values and goals, the true, the good, and the beautiful.'[172]

The Idiosyncratic Alternative

It is interesting to consider the other competitors, apart from Lagerlöf and Swinburne, whom Eucken had been up against, and who were not mentioned by Espmark. Among them was a remarkable and idiosyncratic nomination, the motivation for which remains unclear. The sister of the then deceased philosopher, Friedrich Nietzsche, was nominated: Elisabeth

Förster-Nietzsche. There are only two works by which her nomination could have been justified, the first of which is of questionable objectivity and the second of doubtful authenticity: her *The Life of Friedrich Nietzsche*, first published in German in 1895, and the compilation of various writings under the title *The Will to Power*, published originally in 1901 and in an expanded version in 1906. The man who nominated her was a well-known philosopher in his own right: Hans Vaihinger, who is certainly better known today than Eucken. In 1908 Vaihinger was most renowned for his studies of Kant. The work for which he is most famous would not be published in German until 1911: *The Philosophy of 'As if'*. But in 1902 he had also published a book called *Nietzsche as Philosopher*. He thus had a vested interest in making Nietzsche's name universally known: it would sell more copies of his book.

Elisabeth Förster-Nietzsche was first nominated unsuccessfully by Vaihinger in 1908, but he did not give up that easily, though he did obviously ponder the matter for a few years and tried to drum up a little more support. When he nominated her again in 1916, he had a member of the Swedish Academy to support him, Harald Hjärne no less. In 1917 he went it alone again, but in 1923 he tried for one last time, with three other supporting nominators: Ernst Bertram, a Professor of German Literature in Cologne, Kurt Breysig, Professor of history in Berlin, and the classical philologist, Georg Goetz at the Saxon Academy of Sciences. All to no avail.

We must be thankful however that the Nobel Committee did not take the proposal to give the award to Nietzsche's sister particularly seriously. With hindsight we can see that it would eventually prove very embarrassing for another reason than her dubious scholarship. Would the committee have ever been able to live down the fact that they had awarded the prize to a woman whose husband, Bernhard Förster, a fanatical anti-semite, had attempted to set up a 'pure' Aryan settlement in Paraguay in 1887, with the name 'Nueva Germania'. He committed suicide in 1889, when faced with insurmountable financial problems. Elisabeth later became a supporter of National Socialism and received financial support for her Nietzsche archive from the Nazi government. It is known that Hitler attended her funeral in 1935.

A Philosopher with Élan

Attitudes towards Henri Bergson in 1927 were different from those towards Eucken in 1908, though there were still some reservations about giving the prize to a non-literary recipient. Some committee members were clearly nervous about passing judgement in a field as difficult and complex as philosophy. Österling explained that '…Bergson's inspiring influence on modern literature was a principal motive behind the decision.'[173] Interestingly this seems to have been the feeling of the Academy but not specifically of the Nobel Prize Committee. Espmark is categorical on this, but without citing further evidence: 'The award to Bergson was a decision of the Academy's, against the recommendation of the committee.'[174]

It would seem however that, unlike in the case of Eucken, the Academy got it right with Bergson; esteem for his ideas has only increased with the years. This is not a suitable context to attempt to provide an outline of his complex ideas, though Per Hallström made a brave and adequate effort in his award ceremony speech. He concluded by praising Bergson's celebration of creativity and intuition. Bergson, he said, was a philosopher who, 'as stylist and as poet', in 'breaking the servitude that matter imposes, makes room for idealism.'[175] And thus he fulfilled the main requirement for a Nobel Prize. Nowadays many of his ideas are still influential: especially his writings on causality, time, free will, the perception of change, creativity, laughter, etc. Some of his concepts have become part of general philosophical debate, such as duration, the *élan vital*, and that expounded in the work which won him the Nobel Prize, creative evolution, described by Hallström as 'a cosmogony of great scope and unflagging power, without sacrificing a strictly scientific terminology'.[176]

In his Banquet Speech, delivered for him by the French minister, M. Armand Bernard, Bergson praised the idealism of Nobel, in contrast with most of his contemporaries, and would seem to have had a very idealized view of the committee's procedures himself: 'The prestige of the Nobel Prize is due to many causes, but in particular to its twofold idealistic and international character: idealistic in that it has been designed for works of lofty inspiration; international in that it is awarded after the production of different countries has been minutely studied and the intellectual balance sheet of the whole world has been drawn up.' He lavished praise on the entire Nobel enterprise as '…a foundation with an international character and an idealistic outlook which implies that the entire civilized world is envisaged from a purely intellectual point of view as constituting one single and identical republic of minds. Such is the Nobel Foundation.'[177] Such high praise of the Foundation of course implies that he rated his own accomplishments very highly too!

Fiery Strength and Gay Buoyancy

Bertrand Arthur William Russell, the 3rd Earl Russell, did not rate Bergson as highly as some of his contemporaries. He acknowledged the qualities of his literary style but found his speculations too emotive and not the product of sound reasoning.

Espmark is reticent about the award to Bertrand Russell [1950]. Is it because evaluating such a brilliant analytical mind and lending expression to the committee's reasons for its decision strained its capability? It fell to Österling to justify the choice publicly in the award ceremony speech. It was undoubtedly a wise decision for him to quote Russell's own words on how best to assess a philosopher:

In studying a philosopher, the right attitude is neither reverence nor contempt, but first a kind of hypothetical sympathy, until it is possible to know what it feels like to believe in his theories, and only then should there be a revival of the critical attitude. This should resemble, as far as possible, the state of mind of a person abandoning opinions which he has hitherto held.[178]

He also cites Russell's definition of the role of the philosopher in modern times: 'To teach how to live without certainty, and yet without being paralyzed by hesitation...'[179]

Österling recognizes the complexity and difficulty of Russell's thought, but stresses that what has made him worthy of the Nobel Prize are his efforts to provide readable texts for the non-specialist: 'What is important, from our point of view, is that Russell has so extensively addressed his books to a public of laymen, and, in doing so, has been so eminently successful in keeping alive the interest in general philosophy.' There is also evidence in Russell's writings of a brilliant style, laced with wit. Österling praises 'the sort of dry, fiery strength and gay buoyancy with which he presents his convictions'.[180]

Österling also alludes to Russell as a morally aware animal with a strong political conscience (though he dose not say so in such words): 'Much in Russell's writings excites protest. Unlike many other philosophers, he regards this as one of the natural and urgent tasks of an author.'[181]

And it is the relationship between politics and theory which Russell takes up in his Nobel Lecture ('What Desires are Politically Important?'). More specifically he explores what he feels to be the lack of contemporary discussion of politics and political theory: insufficient account was being taken of psychology.

It is also interesting to note the opposition that Russell was up against in the discussions to decide the award. There were seven nominations for Lagerkvist, six for Churchill, three for Claudel, two each for Mauriac and Greene, with one each for

Broch, Forster, Camus and Sholokhov. There were also nominations for the philosophers Dewey and Jaspers and one for the historian Toynbee. There was thus some quite stiff opposition, and it is worth noting that there was only one nomination for Russell himself.

Proscenium Arch Rivals,
or Eleven Dramatists in Search of a Prize

Many writers of novels and poetry have also dabbled in drama, and some have had not an insignificant success; amongst the Nobel laureates there are many such. Here the focus is to be on those authors who won the award primarily for their talent as dramatists. Thus John Galsworthy [1932] is omitted, though an accomplished dramatist, because his award was primarily for his novels. The same is the case with Günter Grass [1999]. Dario Fo [1997] is in category of his own: although he won the award for his accomplishments in drama, it is in comedy that he has excelled. He is, so far, the only comic writer to have won the award, and will be considered later from this perspective. This is not of course to imply that some of the other dramatists who won the award did not occasionally also write comedies. We are thus left with eleven major dramatists who have managed to upstage all the others, whom they have left languishing in the wings. Their approaches to drama have been as varied as their cultural backgrounds.

Half a Prize for Spanish Flare

The earliest writer to be awarded the prize specifically for drama was also the first to have to share it with another: José Echegaray (sharing with Frédéric Mistral) [1904]. The official justification, in Wirsén's Presentation Speech, for dividing the prize was that it was 'a distinction they both equally merit'.[182] In order to pre-empt speculation that this would devalue the prize, Wirsén stressed that the Academy 'considers each of these two prizes as the equal of the whole prize'.[183] However, what is known of the decision process does not support this equitable interpretation. Espmark's account reveals it to have been a compromise solution to save face and cover up incompetence in a specific part of the process. Apparently the committee had already agreed on Mistral, when they were presented with a rather unsatisfactory translation of one of Mistral's major works produced by one Rupert Nyblom. Wirsén was especially worried about the reputation of the committee if this fact became generally known, and he suggested withdrawing Mistral's candidature and opting instead for Echegaray. But he was only able to ensure that fifty per cent of the committee would be on his side for this proposal. Thus, with the committee at stalemate, they decided to share the prize between the two men. The hope was that they would thus please the admirers of both writers and manage to cover up the embarrassment of having had to consider a poor translation. The problem was therefore resolved for the time being, but as a result of this case there was always scepticism and reluctance concerning proposals for prize-sharing.

There are some hints perhaps in Wirsén's Presentation Speech concerning Echegaray's style that may indicate why, though he may have been popular in the late nineteenth century, his plays have not found a permanent place on the world stage. After an outline of the characteristics of Spanish drama, Wirsén describes Echegaray as 'heir and continuator of these glorious and characteristic traditions'.[184] But the traditions are clearly those of exaggerated melodrama, requiring over-the-top acting: 'In one place, there is brilliant colouring, and in another, a great affection for rhetorical antithesis. Emphatic language is coupled with tangled intrigue. Striking effects are violent, the lyric order intense. Disharmonies are sharp, and conflicts almost always have a tragic resolution.'[185]

The Agnostic Puppeteer

The next author to be honoured primarily for his drama was the Belgian Maurice Maeterlinck [1911]. There is little evidence however of the committee having studied his stage technique or sense of dramatic structure. He was already being considered in 1903, when they were more concerned about his agnosticism and insufficient emphasis on 'man's capacity to determine his life according to moral precepts'.[186] By 1909 Wirsén was beginning to be more sympathetic to Maeterlinck, but still felt the lack of a definite theism, which 'would have had a beneficent influence on his dramatic art'.[187] But by 1909, however, Maeterlinck could be perceived to be emphasizing the aspect of human free will which allowed the possibility of awareness of moral judgements and decisions. The way was being paved for approval in 1911.

It is clear however that the judgement concerning Maeterlinck was based almost entirely on his known moral values and beliefs about human nature, with some consideration of his symbolism in relation to these, rather than on his highly original and significant theory of drama. He believed that no actor could adequately portray the symbolic figures of his plays and came to prefer the use of marionettes, which could better represent how mankind was completely controlled by fate. This led him to develop a theory of 'static drama', expounded in his essay 'The Tragic in Daily Life'. According to this theory his actors were to move and react as if they were marionettes. It is thus clear that the Nobel Committee evaluated Maeterlinck as if he were a moralist, philosopher and a poet, and not as a dramaturge and theorist of the theatre.

A Whiff of the Clinic

The following year, another dramatist received the award: the German author Gerhart Hauptmann [1912]. In 1902 his early work had been condemned by the committee as 'crass natural-ism'. His play *Before Sunrise* was said to contain 'repulsive descrip-tions of drunkenness and vice, even on the verge of incest'. His more symbolic works were said to have 'deeply poetic details' but were also 'hospital-smelling'.[188] By 1912, however, when Erik Axel Karlfeldt became Permanent Secretary of the Academy, the judgements had been greatly revised. The naturalistic dramas were described as 'markedly realistic' and the symbolic works were 'filled with the finest poetry'.[189]

In the Presentation Speech by Hans Hildebrand, the natural-ism had also acquired the idealism which qualified it for the prize: 'The realism in Hauptmann's plays leads necessarily to brighter dreams of new and better conditions and to the wish for their fulfilment.' And a little later he adds; 'Whatever subject he treats, even when he deals with life's seamy side, his is always a noble personality. That nobility and his refined art give his works their wonderful power.'[190]

A Southerner of Negative Virtues

The Prize was awarded to Spain again in 1922 for more of 'the illustrious traditions of Spanish drama'. It seems that in their discussions of Jacinto Benavente, the committee focused mainly on his aesthetic value and only subsequent to that considered if there were any negative aspects to be taken into account. The purpose was to ensure that, as far as the conditions of the will were concerned, there were no obstacles to selecting him. One of the first major points stressed therefore in this respect was 'the negative virtue that he does not promote any doubtful ideals, does not attack any values upon which human life is founded...'[191]

Benavente was in competition with Yeats in 1922. He was lucky in that the committee at that time decided 'to consider the less familiar'.[192] There is also evidence at this time of the committee becoming more aware of the need to recognize a broader inter-national context, 'of the danger of gradually diminishing and specializing the scope of a prize intended to be of world signi-ficance...'[193]

This need to be wary of the committee's own limitations is reflected also in some remarks of Per Hallström in his Presentation Speech. In fact Hallström treads a fine line between a 'northern' and a 'southern' aesthetics. He is not explicit, but there is more than a hint that he finds northern art to be super-ior, richer, profounder: '...Teutonic readers are often reminded, even when it comes to an art as good as this, that it has sprung from a national temperament other than ours and from other poetic traditions. The kind of lyric we desire, at least in the atmosphere of the world of drama, is on the whole probably un-known to the Romance nations. Half-light, both in nature and in the human soul, is lacking in them...' And he adds a little later: 'Their thoughts may have brilliance, rapidity, and, of course, clar-ity; but they strike us as lacking in power, as belonging to a some-what more vacant atmosphere, and as having less life in their inner being.' Then, almost as an afterthought, he adds 'What Southerners say of our art may reveal equally great defects...'[194] It is also very much as if he is saying 'Well, I have heard that he is supposed to be very good, and no doubt Spaniards appreciate his work, but I can't really identify with it at all myself.' What he actually said was that in Benavente's works reflecting com-plex ideas and the unrest of the times '...we cannot follow him with the admiration that has been bestowed upon him by his countrymen'. Indirectly he was saying that his work was provin-cial and could not reach an international audience: 'I have not dwelt on the limitations of his art, but sought to indicate the central qualities of his craftsmanship in his country and in his time.'[195]

On the firmly positive side Hallström did stress Benavente's realism, grace, wide range of subject matter and his qualities as a 'born dramatist': 'He is a rare example of a born dramatist, one whose imagination, by itself, creates in accordance with the laws of the stage, but yet avoids anything theatrical as fully as all other false conventions.'[196]

Bold Archaism

If Benavente beat him to it in 1922, William Butler Yeats did not have to wait very long. He was honoured the very next year. Some account of his role in the development of Irish drama has already been provided in consideration of his creative roots in provincialism; and he devoted his entire Nobel Lecture to 'The Irish Dramatic Movement' focusing particularly on his work with John Synge and Lady Gregory.

In his Presentation Speech, Hallström talked predominantly about his poetry but acknowledged the originality of his drama. After listing some of his poetic dramas, Hallström summed up: 'In these dramatic pieces his verse attains a rare beauty and sureness of style.' Special praise is reserved for *Cathleen ní Houlihan* of 1902, 'which is at once his simplest folk play and his most classically perfect work'. Hallström also made a few observations on Yeats' stage style. His most recent dramas he praised for 'their classic simplicity of form' which developed 'into bold archaism' and also 'the primitive plasticity found in the beginning of all dramatic art'. He stressed that Yeats had devoted himself to 'emancipating himself from the modern stage, with its scenery that disturbs the picture called up by the imagination, with its plays whose features are necessarily exaggerated by the footlights, with its audience's demand for realistic illusion'.[197]

The Intellectual Gladiator

Two years later it was the turn of another Irish dramatist: George Bernard Shaw [1925]. When he had first come up for consideration the committee had been dismissive. In 1911 his play *Mrs Warren's Profession* was regarded as 'downright disturbing because of its subject matter'.[198] Even in the year in which he won the award the committee made the reservation that he had not really produced what could be legitimately called 'dramatic masterpieces'. What was new was to be found in his ideas, and 'not so much in construction and form'. Words like 'intellect', 'directness' and 'freedom' recur in the committee's comments. They saw Shaw's drama as a 'variety of athletics' involving 'gladiatorial exertions'. What made Shaw great was his 'serious and aspiring' intentions.[199]

In his Presentation Speech, Hallström summed up Shaw's way of thinking as 'abstract logical radicalism'. He made people laugh 'so they should not hit upon the idea of hanging him'. He also reiterated the judgement of the committee concerning his dramatic art: 'its novelty does not lie so much in structure and form' but more in 'the directness with which he puts his ideas into practice'. Unique also are 'the bellicosity, the mobility, and the multiplicity of his ideas'.[200]

The Sceptical Psychologist

There have been many condemnations of the committee's choices over the years, but, according to Espmark, there was unusual agreement among critics about the rightness of their selection of Luigi Pirandello [1934], who has continued to be a major influential force in the theatre long after the award.[201]

In his Presentation Speech Hallström devoted a few paragraphs to his novellas and novels, and then focused mainly on his dramas, 'limited as they most often are to purely psychological problems'. Nevertheless he praised 'his almost magical power to turn psychological analysis into good theatre'.[202] The plays have both an extremely narrow focus (on the self and its perceptions) and also a very wide one (on the relativity of all knowledge. While providing some account of other plays, such as *Right You Are (If You Think You Are)* (1917), *The Rules of the Game* (1919), *Henry IV* (1922), *The Life I Gave You* (1924), and others, Hallström reserved special praise for the play *Six Characters in Search of an Author* of 1921: 'The worldwide success of the play, which proves that it has to some extent been understood, is as extraordinary as the piece itself.'[203] Despite finding a negativity in Pirandello's psychology ('The sceptical psychology on which Pirandello has based his remarkable production is purely negative'), Hallström also found a humanity in his writing which enabled him to square the committee's choice with Nobel's requirement of idealism: 'A nobly old-fashioned humanity dominates his ideas about the world of men. His bitter pessimism has not stifled his idealism.'[204]

The Aesthetic Deficiency Syndrome

He was not the first American to win the prize: that honour went to the novelist Sinclair Lewis in 1930. Hallström's comments in his Presentation Speech on Eugene O'Neill [1936] are not without their reservations, but one could not guess at the extent of the disagreement among the committee about him, even by carefully reading between Hallström's lines. Henrik Schück was in the minority in supporting him and when the committee had to meet for a second time in succession but still could not reach a decision, he had to try and win them over. Hallström's specialist report was more negative than his Presentation Speech would lead us to believe. He found in O'Neill's work 'scarcely anything that from start to finish is properly matured'. The committee agreed and found in his work 'effects that do not rest upon means that are essential and legitimate to the drama'. They found that only the first two parts of *Mourning Becomes Electra* had 'the impress of perfection' and some of his other plays gave a 'sometimes totally dispiriting impression'.[205]

Schück, while defending him, also granted some of the objections, agreeing that O'Neill 'undeniably lacks culture' and even his best plays had 'doubtful aesthetic deficiencies'. His argument which eventually won the day was based on O'Neill's 'great poetic force' and 'pure poetic strength'.[206]

With the knowledge of these discussions one can better interpret the reservations in Hallström's award ceremony speech. Thus it can be seen that he focuses entirely on O'Neill's later dramas: 'In his earliest dramas O'Neill was a strict and somewhat arid realist; those works we may here pass by.' In only one of them, *The Moon of the Caribbees* (1918) is he found to attain 'poetic heights'. *Anna Christie* (1921) is praised for its absence of his usual pessimism ('for once pessimism is left out of the picture, the play having what is termed a happy ending'). Hallström clearly did not like at all the expressionistic aspects of O'Neill's plays. This is not especially surprising because Hallström applied a rather eccentric concept of expressionism: 'It endeavours to produce its effects by a sort of mathematical method; it may be said to extract the square root of the complex phenomena of reality, and build with those abstractions a new world on an enormously magnified scale.' Hallström found little to identify with in plays embodying what he understood by expressionism: 'The resulting plays have little connection with real life.'[207]

Hallström was more sympathetic to O'Neill's attempts to emulate classical drama, and Greek tragedy in particular. *Mourning Becomes Electra* (1931) is thus described as 'the author's grandest work'.[208]

Even in his concluding remarks Hallström is ambiguous: 'In choosing Eugene O'Neill as the recipient of the 1936 Nobel Prize in Literature, the Swedish Academy can express its appreciation of his peculiar and rare literary gifts.'[209] The same could be said of the Swedish dramatist for whom O'Neill expressed such admiration and to whom he recognized his own enormous debt in the Banquet Speech read on his behalf: '...I am only too proud of my debt to Strindberg, only too happy to have this opportunity of proclaiming it to his people... And it is my pride to imagine that perhaps his spirit, musing over this year's Nobel award for literature, may smile with a little satisfaction, and find the follower not too unworthy of his Master.'[210]

The Optimist in Extremis

Consideration has already been paid to Jean-Paul Sartre and his famous refusal, but one should also mention in passing that, apart from being an influential philosopher and accomplished novelist, he was also an influential dramatist. Another dramatist, who might be considered as an 'honorary Frenchman' was the Irish-born Samuel Beckett [1969].

It is revealing to observe how the committee, recognizing Beckett's originality, strove to see his work in a positive and optimistic light, presumably so that their choice could be squared with the requirements of Nobel's will. Artur Lundkvist argued that nothingness, in Beckett's work, became 'in a way liberating, stimulating'. Lars Gyllensten argued: 'Beckett is, of course, an optimist – he lays bare the vitality, the creative power that remains when all has been scraped away...'[211]

In the award ceremony speech however Karl Ragnar Gierow made the case more convincingly, managing to start with a witticism: 'mix a powerful imagination with a logic in absurdum, and the result will be either a paradox or an Irishman'.[212] He acknowledged, almost in passing, that Beckett 'has pioneered new modes of expression in fiction and on the stage', but reminds us that his dramatic work also has links with tradition, in particular with French experiments in the latter part of the nineteenth century and especially with Alfred Jarry's *Ubu Roi*. Gierow perceived Beckett's work after the Second World War as essentially a response to the revelations about the extent of human moral depravity practised in the Holocaust. Beckett found hope in the most profoundly negative state of being. His philosophy consisted of 'a negativism that cannot desist from descending to the depths. To the depths it must go because it is only there that pessimistic thought and poetry can work their miracles.'[213] Gierow compared what Beckett accomplished to Aristotle's process of 'catharsis, purification through horror'. He expressed Beckett's accomplishment with a religious metaphor: 'in the realms of annihilation, rises the writing of Samuel Beckett like a miserere from all mankind...' In Beckett's masterpiece, *Waiting for Godot*, he embodies 'man's metaphysical predicament'[214]: a life of waiting for a supreme being about whom nothing is known, and even at the end never comes.

No one has ever been known to express subsequently any doubts about the rightness of the committee's decision in 1969.

The African Eclectic

Wole Soyinka [1986] is of course notable for being the first African to win the Nobel Prize in Literature (born in Nigeria in 1934). In his award ceremony speech Lars Gyllensten paid due attention to the relationship between structures and content in his plays. He has also written poems, novels, an autobiography and many articles and essays, but it is for his plays that he has the greatest renown. Gyllensten pointed out:

It was natural for him to seek this art form, which is closely linked with the African material and with African forms of linguistic and mime creation. His plays make frequent and skilful use of many elements belonging to stage art and which have also genuine roots in African culture-dance and rites, masques and pantomime, rhythm and music, declamation, theatre within the theatre etc.[215]

But Soyinka has also been greatly influenced by Western literature and thought. Gyllensten quoted Soyinka's own definition of his way of working as 'selective eclecticism' and gave due recognition to this in his concluding remarks: '…you have been able to synthesize a very rich heritage from your own country, ancient myths and old traditions, with literary legacies and traditions of European culture.'[216]

In his Banquet Speech Soyinka developed the amusing conceit that the African deity Ogun may have been the progenitor of Alfred Nobel. Ogun was 'the god of creativity and destruction, of the lyric and metallurgy. This deity anticipated your scientist Alfred Nobel at the very beginning of time by clearing a path through primordial chaos, dynamiting his way through the core of earth to open a route for his fellow deities who sought to be reunited with us, mortals.'[217] Here he is jokingly 'undermining' the vanity and presumed superiority of western culture. But in his extensive Nobel Lecture, 'This Past Must Address Its Present', he takes a firmer, more critical stance, especially against racial oppression: 'For there is a gruesome appropriateness in the fact that an African, a black man should stand here today, in the same year that the progressive Prime Minister of his host country was murdered…' And a little later he adds: 'Whatever the facts are about Olof Palme's death, there can be no question about his life. To the racial oppression of a large sector of humanity, Olof Palme pronounced, and acted, a decisive No!'[218]

And if Soyinka was inspired and stimulated by his reading of Western literature, his was also a critical reading: '…how many students of European thought today, even among us Africans, recall that several of the most revered names in European philosophy – Hegel, Locke, Montesquieu, Hume, Voltaire – an endless list – were unabashed theorists of racial superiority and denigrators of the African history and being.' And modes of thought like Marxism he clearly viewed as short-sighted: 'As for the more prominent names among the theorists of revolution and class struggle – we will draw the curtain of extenuation on their own intellectual aberration, forgiving them a little for their vision of an end to human exploitation.'[219]

The Abyss Under Chat

Another dramatist who took the opportunity to use his Nobel Lecture as a political platform was Harold Pinter [2005]. Per Wästberg, in his award ceremony speech, paid due respect to Pinter's political commitments as well as to his accomplishments in the field of drama. He started by focusing on his world renown as a dramatist: 'Harold Pinter is the renewer of English drama in the twentieth-century. "Pinteresque" is an adjective listed in the Oxford Dictionary.' He attempted to characterize the essence of the 'Pinteresque' quality: 'The abyss under chat, the unwillingness to communicate other than superficially, the need to rule and mislead, the suffocating sensation of accidents bubbling under the quotidian, the nervous perception that a dangerous story has been censored – all this vibrates through Pinter's drama.' His characters are 'prisoners in the limbo of class divisions, set phrases and solidified habits'.[220]

Wästberg pointed out that Pinter himself had described even his early plays as political, and suggests that the early works 'can be seen as metaphors for authoritarian intervention on several levels: the power of the state, the power of the family, the power of religion – all undermining the individual's critical questions.' And these characteristics became common to all his writing: 'In a ruthless analysis of the totalitarian, he illuminates the pain of the individual.'[221]

It is clear that, in relation to his plays, Pinter did not regard them as political in any doctrinaire or ideological sense. It was his conviction that the political dimensions had to be allowed to arise naturally from the situation and personalities of the characters. In his Nobel Lecture, 'Art, Truth and Politics', he said:

Political theatre presents an entirely different set of problems. Sermonising has to be avoided at all cost. Objectivity is essential. The characters must be allowed to breathe their own air. The author cannot confine and constrict them to satisfy his own taste or disposition or prejudice. He must be prepared to approach them from a variety of angles, from a full and uninhibited range of perspectives, take them by surprise, perhaps, occasionally, but nevertheless give them the freedom to go which way they will. This does not always work. And political satire, of course, adheres to none of these precepts, in fact does precisely the opposite, which is its proper function.[222]

After examples from some of his plays he then devoted a large part of the lecture to a critical attack on the foreign policy of the United States, especially concerning its involvement in Iraq and Nicaragua.

One cannot leave these reflections on Harold Pinter without some consideration of an extraordinary interview he gave, after the announcement of his Nobel Prize award, and which has been included in its entirety on the Nobel website. The interviewer was the freelance journalist, Marika Griehsel.[223] It must rank as one of the most pointless and insubstantial interviews ever given. It is only eighteen lines long, but for copyright reasons cannot be quoted here in its entirety. When asked about his feelings on hearing the news, Pinter managed only to come up with exclamations of extreme surprise: 'I've been absolutely speechless', 'I'm overwhelmed', 'very deeply moved', 'I'm just bowled over.' When the interviewer attempted to ask him a more specific question about his career, his response was 'I can't answer these questions.' And when he expressed the intention of saying more in Stockholm, the interviewer asked him rather unnecessarily if he would be coming to Stockholm, which he then confirmed. Then the interviewer thanked him, to which he replied 'Okay?' They then thanked each other several times. And that was it. The question naturally arises why it was decided to include this particularly fatuous interview on the Nobel website. The most generous interpretation is that the intention was to confirm Wästberg's interpretation of the 'Pinteresque' as 'the abyss under chat, the unwillingness to communicate other than superficially', and perhaps to demonstrate that Pinter's style was essentially realistic: he was just writing in the way he normally talked to others.

Profundity or Obscurity?
And The Challenges of Translation

Poetry is poetry, and prose is prose, but the twain quite often meet and can become indistinguishable. It is a poem, if you say it is a poem: otherwise it is prose. And if you are not sure you can call it a prose poem or poetic prose. The Nobel Committee has found itself in deep water concerning such matters over the years. While preferring the clear-cut and simple, it has obviously found itself at times confused by complexity. But then aren't we all?

Prize-winning poets themselves have not been unaware of these problems. The truly good poet does not want to be incomprehensible, or what is the point of writing? Pablo Neruda [1971] in his Nobel Lecture, 'Towards the Splendid City', said:

> ...if we succeed in creating the fetish of the incomprehensible (or the fetish of that which is comprehensible only to a few), the fetish of the exclusive and the secret, if we exclude reality and its realistic degenerations, then we find ourselves suddenly surrounded by an impossible country, a quagmire of leaves, of mud, of cloud, where our feet sink in and we are stifled by the impossibility of communicating.[224]

The Poet and the Scientist

In his Banquet Speech in 1960, Saint-John Perse explored the common ground of poetry and scientific imagination and thus creation, and asked '...is one not justified in considering the tool of poetry as legitimate as that of logic?' And he added a little later: '...in as much as there exists an equivalence between the modes of sensibility and intellect, it is the same function that is exercised initially in the enterprises of the poet and the scientist.'[225]

He defended poetry against accusations of obscurity, on the grounds that obscurity is not characteristic of poetry but of that which it explores, and poetry endeavours to make clear what is obscure: 'The obscurity for which it is reproached pertains not to its own nature, which is to illuminate, but to the night which it explores, the night of the soul and the mystery in which human existence is shrouded. Obscurity is banished from its expression and this expression is no less exacting than that of science.'[226]

The Joys of DIY

Various members of the Nobel Committee, and at times the committee in general, have at times revealed their perplexity in the face of understanding profound and complex poets. How they nevertheless reached decisions in the end can serve an object lesson.

The task of selection has of course been complicated by the fact that most of the poetry has had to be studied and assessed in translation. The task was made easier on the occasion of the committee's award to Rabindranath Tagore [1913]: Tagore produced his own translations of his poems. Of Tagore's *Song Offerings*, Harald Hjärne said, in his award ceremony speech:

Since last year the book, in a real and full sense, has belonged to English literature, for the author himself, who by education and practice is a poet in his native Indian tongue, has bestowed upon the poems a new dress, alike perfect in form and personally original in inspiration. This has made them accessible to all in England, America, and the entire western world for whom noble literature is of interest and moment.[227]

One cannot help wondering however whether the committee would have looked so favourably on Tagore if he had not had the might of the British Empire behind him: 'Tagore has been hailed from various quarters as a new and admirable master of that poetic art which has been a never-failing concomitant of the expansion of British civilization ever since the days of Queen Elizabeth.'[228] It is clear that the committee's favourable decision depended very much on the quality of Tagore's translations of his own work, '…the choice of words and his use of the other elements of expression in a borrowed tongue.' His stories they were forced to judge by someone else's translations: 'Though the form of these tales does not bear his own stamp – the rendering being by another hand – their content gives evidence of his versatility and wide range of observation.'[229]

A Dead Poet's Society

One cannot help wondering whether Erik Axel Karlfeldt's success in 1931 had something to do with his being Swedish, not to mention the fact that he was also a member of the Swedish Academy. There is of course no reason why the Swedish Academy should not chose a Swedish poet, but it smacks of honouring a colleague's memory, because at the time of the award Karlfeldt was already dead. It has been the only case so far of the award being made posthumously, which is strictly speaking against the stipulations of Nobel's will. Karlfeldt had been an active member of the Nobel Committee for many years. He had been elected in 1904 and became its permanent secretary in 1912.

He had refused the award several times in his lifetime, according to Espmark, though of course finally in 1931, having departed this world, he was not in a position to object. Little can now be unearthed about the committee's deliberations on that occasion, because, as Espmark points out, none of the discussions about other members of the committee is ever documented. However one can be sure that a decisive factor would have been the fact that the committee members would have had no problems with obscurities in his work: they all understood his language perfectly well. And there was 'no disqualifying "difficulty" in his work'.[230]

In his Presentation Speech, Österling sounds a little defensive, when he resorts to the irrefutable argument that without a knowledge of Swedish it is impossible to appreciate Karlfeldt qualities as a poet (though the committee was of course quite happy to evaluate foreign poets in translation):

It is the deliberate self-limitation of lyrical poetry, and at the same time its fate, that its most profound qualities and values are indissolubly connected with the character and rhythm of its original language, with the meaning and weight of every single word. Karlfeldt's individuality may be dimly felt in translation, but only in Swedish can it be fully comprehended.[231]

At the banquet Prof. C.W. Oseen put his finger on the painful truth of the situation: 'Out of the prize meant to help a needy artist we have made a wreath to adorn the coffin of our most beloved poet.'[232]

Translation as Recreation

In his Banquet Speech, T.S. Eliot focused on the problems of understanding poetry and the unavoidable necessity of translation. We have noted already his comment, 'Poetry is usually considered the most local of arts.' And he added: 'Poetry, it might seem, separates peoples instead of uniting them.' But he argued that we should try to overcome these limitations: '...poetry itself gives us a reason for trying to overcome the barrier.' The translation of poetry can never be a direct word-for-word rendering. In Eliot's words, it must be for each poet 'a kind of recreation of his poems by other poets'.[233]

And almost as though it were in response to Österling's remarks concerning Karlfeldt, Eliot added: 'In the work of every poet there will certainly be much that can only appeal to those who inhabit the same region, or speak the same language, as the poet.'[234]

The Mystique of the Individual

The poet Salvatore Quasimodo [1959], in his Nobel Lecture, 'The Poet and the Politician', views the issue of the translation of poetry in a more complex way and shows awareness at the same time of some necessary quality of obscurity in poetry. For him the poet is the only person who can revive a written language. The language of the poet is of necessity difficult because of what he is trying to express: 'His language is difficult not because of philological reasons or spiritual obscurity, but because of its content.' He also made the challenging assertion: 'Poets can be translated; men of letters cannot...'[235] By 'men of letters' he clearly meant essentially epigones, writers who express 'derivative thought'. One wonders whether some members of the Nobel Committee were shifting uneasily in their seats when he added: 'Men of letters think of Europe or even of the whole world in the light of a poetics that isolates itself, as if poetry were an identical "object" all over the world.' For Quasimodo, a poet 'clings to his own tradition and avoids internationalism.' Men of letters, on the other hand, always seek a familiar content: '...formalistic men of letters may prefer certain kinds of content and violently reject others. But the problem on either side of the barricade is always content.' But this content, which the poetry is trying to express, is the most individual and therefore difficult to access: 'The poet's spoken discourse often depends on a mystique, on the spiritual freedom that finds itself enslaved on earth.'[236]

Master of Monotony

The committee was equally reliant upon translations to read the work of Greek poet, Giorgos Seferis [1963]. He was, according to Österling in his award ceremony speech, 'acclaimed abroad in so far as his poetry has been made available in translation'.[237] Conveniently for Seferis, his work had been available in Swedish translation for thirteen years already (as acknowledged by Österling). But nevertheless the committee seems to have yielded to the fact that his talent had been generally recognized, rather than to his comprehensibility: 'His poetry sometimes seems difficult to interpret, particularly because Seferis is reluctant to expose his inner self, preferring to hide behind a mask of anonymity.' Österling quoted a remark by Seferis however, which should have provided the committee with some reassurance: 'I am a monotonous and obstinate man who, for twenty years, has not ceased to say the same things over and over again.'[238]

Too Difficult By Half

There were many other poets however who were not allowed to get away with being difficult. The committee was unequivocal in its dismissal of Paul Valéry in their discussions from 1930 onwards. They found that with the years he had become more and more inaccessible ('a difficulty seemingly intended'). The committee felt that they could not be answerable to the public if it gave the award to Valéry. They would not be able to 'meet with equanimity the quite natural bewilderment of that public over the recognition of an author whose work is so inaccessible'. They doubted if his poetry could be 'assumed to retain a lasting quality beyond the experimental'.[239] There were similar dismissive discussions about the German poets, Arno Holz, in 1929, and Stefan George, in 1931, as well as Paul Claudel, in 1937.

Assessing the Inscrutable

In 1968, in their first award to an East Asian writer, Yasunari Kawabata, the committee was clearly nervous of their understanding of someone who 'expresses the essence of the Japanese mind',[240] whatever the characteristics of that mind might be. They had clearly done all that they were capable of before making their final selection. The process, from proposal to decision, took seven years. In 1961 a Swedish critic studied a number of his works, but he had to do so in a very indirect way: through translations into French, German and English. Two American scholars, who were experts in Japanese literature, were also consulted, as was the Japanese scholar Sei Ito. The members of the committee also managed to read several of the works in Swedish translation.[241]

In his Nobel Lecture, 'Japan, the Beautiful and Myself', Kawabata attempted to convey something of the obscure philosophy behind Japanese aesthetics, considering mainly poetry but also the visual art of calligraphy (an art form in China, Japan and Korea, which, due to its dependence on an intimate knowledge of the written languages and related pictograms, is generally inaccessible to the sensitivities of most Westerners). He cited a famous poem by the poet Myoe, which, without the Japanese calligraphy and its associations, comes across in English as a mere sequence of ejaculations:

Bright, bright, and bright, bright, bright, and bright, bright.
Bright and bright, bright, and bright, bright moon.[242]

The Poem as Makeshift Answer

There are many cases in which it is far better to read what the original poet has said, rather than ponder on the significance of all those commentaries by critics and Nobel Committee members. This is certainly the case with Wistawa Szymborska [1996].

In her award ceremony speech Mrs Birgitta Trotzig, in spite of the difficulty, attempted to provide some account of Szymborska's greatness, but found it impossible to avoid phrases of almost meaningless ambiguity. She talked of Szymborska's 'wonderful dramaturgy of the world' and the 'many capricious harlequin languages of transformation and identification'. She claimed: 'In Szymborska's surface is depth' and in her 'path of negation' she found 'a quiet but tremendous explosion of being'. One can, apparently, feel in her poetry 'the world's obtrusive unambiguousness being transformed'.[243] Szymborska herself, in her Nobel Lecture, 'The Poet and the World', is much more modest in attempting to describe what she is doing in her poetry, and therefore much clearer and more convincing: 'Poets, if they're genuine, must also keep repeating "I don't know." Each poem marks an effort to answer this statement, but as soon as the final period hits the page, the poet begins to hesitate, starts to realize that this particular answer was pure makeshift that's absolutely inadequate to boot.'[244]

A Poisonous Mumble

Although this section has been concerned exclusively with the works of poets, it is, in conclusion, instructive to draw some links with prose writers, who can also be obscure and so poetic that one is tempted to risk the generalization that perhaps the only indisputable difference between prose and poetry is that the former is 'joined up writing' and the latter is not. There will be some consideration of Elfriede Jelinek [2004] as a novelist later, but here she features as yet another occasion for a member of the committee to attempt the impossible task of defining a writer whom he, Horace Engdahl, clearly found incomprehensible. He opened his award ceremony speech with the words: 'What first perplexes when reading Elfirede Jelinek is the strange, mixed voice that speaks from her writing.' She 'captures, hidden behind common sense, a poisonous mumble of no origin or address.' He talked also of her 'instrumentation of heartless word-plays, macabre metaphors and infernally twisted quotations from the classics'. The reader has to work very hard indeed to gain any insight: 'The difficulty in reading Elrfiede Jelinek is that there is no sympathetic narrator in whom the reader can rest and with whom the reader can identify. It is an awakening from the narcissism of reading.'[245]

If it was intended as a compliment, Engdahl's remark addressed directly to Jellinek at the end of his speech could be interpreted as a reproach: 'You negotiate with neither society nor your time, nor do you adapt to your readers.'[246]

The Novel Lumbers On, or
The Genre That Would Not Die

Realism and the Grand Style

In the context of the Nobel Prize in Literature there seems to have been little reflection, in the early years at least, on the status and viability of the novel as a genre. Very much alive and kicking seems to have been the general consensus of opinion. But the criteria for the kinds of novels which have been regarded as truly great have changed frequently over the years. In the early years, especially under Wirsén, the watchwords were still very much 'realism' and the 'grand style'. Thus in 1910 the committee described the German laureate Paul Heyse as nothing short of a genius: 'Germany has not had a greater literary artist since Goethe.' But by 1967 the critic Theodore Ziolkowski was able to describe the selection of Heyse as one of the committee's greatest mistakes.[247] The blame cannot be put entirely at the feet of Wirsén however. As he said in his Presentation Speech: 'The Swedish Academy has awarded it to a writer whose nomination has been supported by more than sixty German experts on art, literature, and philosophy.'[248]

There was some hesitation about the award to the French writer Rollain Rolland in 1915 for his novel *Jean-Christophe*. The majority of members were in favour of Pérez Galdós, and Hjärne especially criticized strongly the proposal to consider Rolland. He found the novel 'somewhat formless' and disliked the whole genre of 'artist's novel'. The final report of the committee had only two members in favour of Rolland, but the Academy overruled this and selected Rolland.[249]

The 1920 prize went to the Norwegian writer, Knut Hamsun, primarily for his novel *Growth of the Soil* of 1917. Clearly the committee believed they had rewarded a universally acclaimed modern classic of realist novel-writing. In his Presentation Speech Hjärne said that it was 'a book that in a short time has spread everywhere in its original form or in translation. Through the originality of its plot and style, it has aroused the liveliest interest in many countries and has found favourable reception with the most diverse groups of readers.' But if the novel was realist in character, Hjärne perceived that Hamsun had written in accordance with the principles of Nobel by creating as the main character 'the ideal labourer'.[250]

In his Banquet Speech Hamsun expressed in simple words the essential truth about all good writing, that it should be uniquely tailored to the individual: 'A distinguished speaker said earlier tonight that I have my own way of writing, and this much I may perhaps claim and no more.'[251]

There was considerable disagreement about the choice of the French author, Anatole France, in 1921, with Hjärne rejecting France and preferring Galsworthy. Schück, on the other hand, praised France as 'a true humanist' and 'the greatest stylist in modern France'.[252] Special praise was reserved by E.A. Karlfeldt in his Presentation Speech for one of his novels: *At the Sign of the Reine Pédauque* (1893). Convincing realism in the depiction of characters was the keynote: 'There he has sketched a group of true-to-life characters, legitimate or natural offspring of his mind in their own colourful world.'[253]

Although only three members voted for another Norwegian writer, Sigrid Unset, in 1928, the Academy opted for her. While praising her gifts of character depiction, the official report also found her to be guilty of 'confused composition' and 'a certain monotony'. It is reported that Schück found that her psychology was neither ancient nor modern and predicted that it would not be long before no one was reading her works.[254] Hallström was also unable to refrain from some negative remarks in his Presentation Speech. He pointed out that she projected feminist views into an age when they were unknown: 'In medieval documents, the feminist question is not known; one never finds hints of the inner personal life which later was to raise this question. The historian, demanding proofs, has the right to note this discrepancy.' And even within the same sentence he praised and condemned her: 'Her narrative is vigorous, sweeping, and at times heavy.'[255]

Undset was followed by an author now regarded indisputably as having greatness, but about whom there was some disagreement at the time of the award: the German novelist, Thomas Mann. He was first discussed by the committee in 1924, and they failed to agree in their assessment of Mann's novel *Buddenbrooks*. It was decided to await publication of his later work. Hallström praised him highly, but Schück and Karlfeldt disagreed with him. In the final report in 1929, Mann's latest novel, *The Magic Mountain*, was not even mentioned. In the report it was *Buddenbrooks* again which was singled out as 'a masterpiece in the tradition of bourgeois novel-writing'.[256] And in the Presentation Speech by Fredrik Böök realism was again the key: 'Here is the first and as yet unsurpassed German realistic novel in the grand style'[257], (Böök seems not to have known of the great Prussian novelist admired by Mann, Theodore Fontane, whose novels influenced *Buddenbrooks* in particular).

The Honorary Swede

The American novelist Sinclair Lewis [1930] was lucky. American he may have been, strictly speaking, but he was also an honorary Swede, according to Karlfeldt in his Presentation Speech. He was 'a native of a part of America which for a long time has had

Swedish contacts'. Karlfeldt described his major novels at length, starting with *Main Street* (1920), in which the prairies have 'winters, long and cold as ours'. And he adds 'To be sure, the town is first and foremost American, but it could, as a spiritual milieu, be situated just as well in Europe.' Of one of Lewis' most famous novels, *Elmer Gantry* (1927), Karlfeldt admitted that it had aspects unfamiliar to a European: 'To what extent a pulpiteer like Elmer Gantry is common over there, we cannot here have the slightest idea.' Finally, Karlfeldt invited his audience to consider the fact that (in 1930) American literature was still young, adolescent indeed, not yet mature, like the nation itself. But his 'end of term' report is promising: it could do well. The prospects are good: 'The new great American literature has started with national self-criticism. It is a sign of health.' And Lewis himself 'has the manners of a new settler, who takes new land into cultivation. He is a pioneer.'[258]

At the banquet, another member of the Swedish Academy, Tor Hedberg, felt it necessary to consider some of the criticisms that had been made of their choice of an American that year. Given the sensitivity revealed over the years by many Americans concerning a perceived European bias in the selection of laureates, it is worth quoting his words, spoken directly to Lewis, at length:

It has been said that the Nobel Prize in Literature has found its way across the Atlantic far too late. If so, it has not been due to any indifference on the part of the Swedish Academy, nor to any lack of knowledge, but rather to an 'embarras de richesses'. It has further been said that the award of a prize to your work, in which the follies of mankind – not excluding those that are perhaps special to America – have been scourged, is an expression of some kind of European or Swedish animosity against America. I dare to assert that this is a complete mistake.[259]

Sagas: The Doubtful Art Form

The British author John Galsworthy has already been mentioned in relation to his contribution to drama, but the major work cited in the Presentation Speech by Österling was his popular sequence of novels, *The Forsyte Saga*. The first volume had appeared in 1906, and it was not until 1918 that he took up the family history again. One of the features of the saga which drew the admiration and praise of the committee was the way in which it revealed how the author's thought had changed and matured in the course of the sequence of novels. Österling commented: 'The radical critic of culture rises by degrees to a greater objectivity in his appreciation and to a more liberal view of the purely human.'[260]

Another 'saga' won the prize for its author in 1937. The award to the French author, Roger Martin du Gard, was mainly for his sequence of novels, *Les Thibault* (1922–40). He had been under consideration since 1935, but the committee decided to delay its judgement till the series of novels was complete. Apart from the epilogue it was finished by 1936. But the discussion was not free from complications. Hallström believed that the giant serial novel was 'a doubtful art form'. He found that the author included too much realistic detail and indulged in too frequent psychologizing. Österling, who recognized some weaknesses, praised its 'psychological richness' and 'universal interest' (the buzzword of that period of the Academy's history).[261]

It was Hallström who made the award ceremony speech however, and some of his reservations can be glimpsed in his phrasing. He describes the series of novels as a 'roman fleuve': 'a narrative method that is relatively little concerned with composition and advances like a river across vast countries, reflecting everything that is found on its way'. He further describes the essence of such novels as consisting in 'the exactitude of this reflection rather than in the harmonious balance of its parts: it has no shape'. His compliments are very backhanded: 'Nevertheless, the novel is there, with its boundless substance...' and

'The reader's aesthetic demands will be satisfied in isolated sections of the work which are more condensed and therefore better suited to call forth his feelings. *Les Thibault* does not lack such sections.' There are many other examples of Hallström's praise with implied criticism in the rest of his speech.[262]

To give him his due, it is worth quoting at length du Gard's own defence of the 'born novelist', which he made in his Banquet Speech in the context of references to 'the immortal example of Tolstoy':

> The born novelist recognizes himself by his passion to penetrate ever more deeply into the knowledge of man and to lay bare in each of his characters that individual element of his life which makes each being unique. It seems to me that any chance of survival which a novelist's work may have rests solely on the quantity and the quality of the individual lives that he has been able to create in his books. But that is not all. The novelist must also have a sense of life in general; his work must reveal a personal vision of the universe. Here again Tolstoy is the great master.[263]

Popular But Limited

The choice of the American writer Pearl Buck in 1938 caused a bit of a stir. Espmark describes her as 'an author of limited caliber yet universal range' and felt that the selection had been conducted in haste.[264] In the report of 8th September one member was in favour of Buck, with the majority in favour of the Finn Stijn Streuvels, and Österling rooting for Hermann Hesse. Eventually the Academy, not the committee, voted on a minority report of 19th September. In this case there was not the customary several years' wait to see if she truly qualified.

It is possible that the decision to choose a popular novelist was influenced by the fact that in the same year the committee had to consider a proposal for the author of *Gone with the Wind*, Margaret Mitchell. Espmark comments that the episode shows up a weakness in the whole selection procedure, which would-be laureates around the world would do well to take note of: 'there is a significant degree of incompetence among those who, in various parts of the world, have the right to nominate candidates because of the positions they hold'.[265]

In her Nobel Lecture, Pearl Buck provided a perceptive account of the development of prose fiction in China, with some reflections on her own kind of realism, which, she said, must be spontaneously created and not out of concern for aesthetic ideals: 'The defining of art, therefore, is a secondary and not a primary process. And when one born for the primary process of creation, as the novelist is, concerns himself with the secondary process, his activity becomes meaningless.'[266]

It is interesting to note that in her Banquet Speech she acknowledges the fact that American literature had not yet fulfilled completely its promise:

I accept, too, for my country, the United States of America. We are a people still young and we know that we have not yet come to the fullest of our powers. This award, given to an American, strengthens not only one, but the whole body of American writers, who are encouraged and heartened by such generous recognition.[267]

The perceptive reader will have noticed echoes here of the comments by Tor Hedberg on Sinclair Lewis.

A Pioneer, an Innovator and an Experimenter

The Swiss author Hermann Hesse [1946] was actually proposed by another laureate, Thomas Mann, and he was first discussed in 1931. For some time he was felt to be lacking what the committee deemed requisite qualities: there was evidence of 'ethical anarchy' in his work, and his characterization was felt to be deficient in many respects. By 1939 the committee still felt unable to call him 'a poet of truly great stature'. If one accepts the thesis that neutrality is also a political stance, then, given the fact that Europe was at war, Österling's and Fogelqvist's minority report in that year was also a political argument: '…Hermann Hesse in his capacity as a non-political author is moreover a worthy and sympathetically original representative of beleaguered but persistent humanism.'[268] But Hesse's time had still not yet come. It was especially thanks to Österling's strong support that Hesse was successful in 1946. It was a period in which innovators and pioneers were favoured, and Hesse at last fitted the bill. The enthusiasm for Hesse can be perceived in Österling's award ceremony speech. Hesse's novel *Der Steppenwolf* (famous enough under its German title not to need translation), a fantastic dreamlike creation, came in for particular praise.

The French author André Gide [1947] was very much aware that he was a replacement for the committee's original choice, Paul Valéry, who inconveniently died in July 1945. The committee had obviously come a long way since their decision in 1931 to make the award to their beloved fellow Swede, Erik Axel Karlfeldt, although he too had had the lack of foresight to quit this life before his colleagues could make a decision. In the Banquet Speech read out for Gide, by the French ambassador, he expressed his admiration for Valéry 'whose death alone prevents you from electing him in my place'.[269] Gide was however found by some members to be a provocative writer, but he won the day for being an innovator and experimenter. The work of his which came in for special praise was *The Counterfeiters* of 1926. Österling said of it in his award ceremony speech: 'Through the novelty of its technique, this novel has inspired a whole new orientation in the contemporary art of the narrative.'[270]

The prize for the American William Faulkner in 1949 was not actually presented to him till the ceremony in 1950. He too was revered as a great experimenter, as Gustav Hellström put it in his Presentation Speech: 'Moreover – side by side with Joyce and perhaps even more so – Faulkner is the greatest experimentalist among twentieth-century novelists. Scarcely two of his novels are similar technically.' (Joyce was one of the most lamented omissions by the Nobel Committee in their awards, but in fact no one had ever nominated him). He was also felt to be incomparable in his psychological insight: 'With almost every new work Faulkner penetrates deeper into the human psyche', and 'as a probing psychologist he is the unrivalled master among all living British and American novelists.'[271]

Scandinavian or Not

It must have been extremely difficult to be completely objective, when the committee selected one of its own members, Pär Lagerkvist, for the prize in 1951 (Lagerkvist was elected to the Swedish Academy in 1940). Espmark mentions the matter only a few times and with discretion. The committee must certainly have been aware of the likelihood of some international reaction to the choice of a Swede, and Österling, in his award ceremony speech, attempted to some extent to pre-empt this. Drawing attention to Nobel's stipulation that the prizes should be awarded 'without any consideration of nationality, so that they should be awarded to the worthiest, be he Scandinavian or not', Österling pointed out that being Swedish should therefore logically 'not in the end hinder him from obtaining it'. He further supported their choice by stressing that there had been much advocacy of his case from abroad: '…his last work has attracted much sympathy and esteem outside our frontiers. This was further proved by the insistent recommendations with which Lagerkvist's candidacy has been sustained by a majority of foreign advisers. He does not owe his prize to the Academy circle itself.'[272]

The particular work which seems to have consolidated Lagerkvist's reputation abroad is the novel *Barabbas* (1950), 'which is all the more remarkable as the style of it is original and in a sense untranslatable'. Nevertheless it had somehow commended itself to the world: 'This reminds us once more that regional individuality can sometimes be transformed into something universal and accessible to all.'[273] Österling's defence therefore reveals that the committee still seem to have been working with an unspoken, perhaps undefined and even unconscious notion of a supreme European standard for literature.

Lagerkvist had, perhaps wisely, refrained from making a long speech at the banquet and read instead a literary text written by himself. He was at pains however to point out that he at no time influenced the committee's deliberations: 'Having taken no part in making this decision, however, I can enjoy it with a free conscience. The responsibility rests with my esteemed colleagues and for this, too, I am truly thankful!'[274]

The Power of Otherness

In his award ceremony speech for the French author François Mauriac [1952], Österling drew attention to an aspect of his writing which we have discovered in this book to be common to many Nobel laureates: the transformation of regional, provincial life into something which acquires a universal significance: 'this writer, who is read the world over, is undeniably and markedly a man of the province, but his provincialism does not exclude the great human problems of universal scope'. It is the same with his Catholicism, which may appear alien to some readers, but which again reflects universal concerns. Österling first praised Mauriac's journalism, but the reason he was awarded the Nobel Prize 'is obviously above all because of his admirable novels'. Österling listed the major novels but did not single out any particular one. He praised Mauriac's 'conciseness and expressive force of language' and his ability to 'in a few suggestive lines shed light on the most complex and difficult things'.[275]

The central role of regionalism in the greatest literature was taken up by Mauriac himself in his Banquet Speech. He reminded his listeners that the strength and power of the greatest writers always actually resides in their very otherness, in their ability to enable us to recognize ourselves in beings of completely different cultures:

> …we forget that the books which enchanted us, the novels of George Eliot or Dickens, of Tolstoy or Dostoevsky, or of Selma Lagerlöf, described countries very different from ours, human beings of another race and another religion. But nonetheless we loved them only because we recognized ourselves in them. The whole of mankind is revealed in the peasant of our birthplace, every countryside of the world in the horizon seen through the eyes of our childhood. The novelist's gift consists precisely in his ability to reveal the universality of this narrow world into which we are born, where we have learned to love and to suffer.[276]

A Life of Eternal Striving

There have been some speculations on political aspects of the choice of Ernest Hemingway in 1954, fuelled very much by the remarks of one of the Academy members: Dag Hammarskjöld. It seems that Hemingway had in fact been a candidate for some time, and that it was recognition of his masterpiece *The Old Man and the Sea* (1952) that decided the committee in his favour. Espmark is categorical: 'I have not found the slightest hint of a political intention behind the 1954 decision, neither in the reports nor in correspondence, nor in any other material.'[277]

The remarks by Hammarskjöld which sparked the whole thing off were made in the late fifties. He was reflecting in a letter to Sten Selander, of 12th May 1955, on some of the decisions made when he first joined the committee in that year. The following well-known remark has already been cited in another context: 'Churchill-Hemingway-Sholokhov: is the Swedish Academy a literary committee in the Foreign Office?'[278] It seems that he felt that the Academy was being pressurized to show favours to countries it needed to get on well with.

The picture is further complicated by other kinds of speculations that have been prompted by a more recently published book: *Spies: The Rise and Fall of the KGB in America*. The book was co-written by John Earl Haynes, Harvey Klehr and Alexander Vassiliev. Vassiliev had been a KGB officer, who had been given access in the nineties to intelligence archives in Moscow from the Stalin period. The book claims that Hemingway was working as a spy for the Russians in the 1940s, though firm evidence has not been forthcoming. Any whiff of such activity in the early 1950s would certainly have put the cat among the pigeons in the Swedish Academy.

In Österling's award ceremony speech there is certainly no glimmer of political considerations. The emphasis was entirely on Hemingway's skills as a writer. If *The Old Man and the Sea* was the work which tipped the balance, then it was mainly for his body of novels that the prize was awarded.

Österling stressed the Americanism of Hemingway's writing, and it was this, he believed, which made him popular with the European public: 'It was the general wish that Americans should write as Americans, thereby making their own contribution to the contest in the international arena.' However it is hard not to perceive a slight note of condescension still in his comment: 'Ernest Hemingway, more than any of his American colleagues, makes us feel that we are confronted by a still young nation which seeks and finds its exact form of expression.'[279]

In his Banquet Speech (read for him by the United States Ambassador to Sweden, John C. Cabot), Hemingway set forth some hard and very demanding challenges for the would-be great writer: 'Writing, at its best, is a lonely life. Organizations for writers palliate the writer's loneliness but I doubt if they improve his writing. He grows in public stature as he sheds his loneliness and often his work deteriorates. For he does his work alone and if he is a good enough writer he must face eternity, or the lack of it, each day.' And for him writing should also always be an eternal striving for something he fears may be beyond his capabilities: 'For a true writer each book should be a new beginning where he tries again for something that is beyond attainment. He should always try for something that has never been done before or that others have tried and failed. Then sometimes, with great luck, he will succeed.'[280]

Bearing Witness

The award to the French author Albert Camus in 1957 was mainly on the strength of his two major novels, *The Stranger* (1942) and *The Plague* (1947). His then most recent work, *The Fall* (1956) obviously won the committee round. In his award ceremony speech Österling praised these three works especially, emphasizing that they had been written 'using an art with complete classical purity of style and intense concentration'.[281] In his Banquet Speech Camus emphasized how he could not live without writing but how also he could not exist apart from humanity. He wrote to become involved:

> For myself, I cannot live without my art. But I have never placed it above everything. If, on the other hand, I need it, it is because it cannot be separated from my fellow men, and it allows me to live, such as I am, on one level with them. It is a means of stirring the greatest number of people by offering them a privileged picture of common joys and sufferings. It obliges the artist not to keep himself apart; it subjects him to the most humble and the most universal truth.[282]

The Guatemalan author Miguel Ángel Asturias won the prize in 1967 very much on the basis of his innovative approach to narrative. Österling expressed the view in his award ceremony speech that 'Asturias has completely freed himself from obsolete narrative techniques. Very early, he came under the influence of the new tendencies appearing in European literature; his explosive style bears close kinship to French surrealism.' Particular praise is bestowed by Öterling on Asturias' famous novel, *The President*, of 1946, but also on a trilogy of novels published between 1950 and 1960.[283] In his Nobel Lecture ('The Latin American Novel, Testimony of an Epoch'), Asturias was firm about the seriousness of the job of novel-writing: 'If you write novels merely to entertain – then burn them!' A writer's work will not last if the aim is only to entertain: 'Just consider how many writers there have been who – down the ages – have written novels to entertain! And who remembers them now? On the other hand, how easy it is to repeat the names of those amongst us who have written to bear witness.'[284]

In 1972 there was considerable discussion within what was then still West Germany suggesting that there had been political motivation in the choice of Heinrich Böll, that it was in some way expressing support for the Social Democratic Party in Germany, with which Böll was closely associated. But again Espmark could find no evidence of this in the Academy's records.[285] In an earlier section of the present book there has been some discussion of Böll in relation to the theme of homelessness. And his treatment of this theme is cited in Karl Ragnar Gierow's Presentation Speech as one of the major features of his work which won him the prize. Gierow identified twin themes running throughout Böll's work of homelessness and 'the aesthetic of the humane'. He traced it throughout his work, culminating in what he called his 'magnum opus', *Group Portrait with a Lady* (1971), 'which so far crowns his work'. Gierow also praised his ironical use of a nineteenth century style of realism, and his economical, pared down use of language. Above all it was not as an experimenter that he was being honoured however but as one who was contributing greatly to 'the renewal of German Literature' after the devastation of the Second World War.[286]

A New Continent

In 1973 the prize went to the Antipodes. In the newspaper *Stockholms-Tidningen* of 26th May 1962, a certain Artur Lundkvist introduced the Swedish people to the works of the Australian Patrick White. In 1968 Lundkvist was elected to the Swedish Academy, and in 1973 he made the speech at the award ceremony, on the occasion of White's winning the prize.

The brief citations published by the Academy on the announcement of an award do not always reveal the happiest choice of words. In White's case it was for 'his epic and psychological narrative art which has introduced a new continent into literature'. This could of course be interpreted, and indeed was so by many, as implying that Australia had been lacking in literature before White appeared on the scene. Lundkvist promptly attempted to dispel such misinterpretations in his speech: such words 'should not be taken to deny the existence of an important body of Australian literature apart from his writings'.[287]

Lundkvist praised the ways in which White transcended 'the local and the national' but admitted that he was a rather difficult writer: 'In his broad narrative he uses a highly compressed language, a verbal art worked out to the last detail and constantly aiming for a maximum of expressive effect, a relentless intensification or a subtle penetration.'[288]

A Hovel for the Spirit

In 1976 it was the turn of an American again. Saul Bellow was praised by Gierow in his award ceremony speech for making a new departure in the American novel, away from the 'hard-boiled style, with its virile air and choppy prose' which had by then 'slackened into an everyday routine'. Bellow had started by dipping back most of all into the refined nineteenth-century realism of Maupassant and Flaubert, and the *fin de siècle* Henry James. Then he started to feature many anti-heroes, men trying to find their foothold in an unstable world, and Gierow found especially that his novel *Seize the Day* (1956) was 'one of the classic works of our time'. Gierow recounted that writing was for Bellow something akin to a religious experience. In an interview Bellow had talked of having access to 'a primitive prompter or commentator within, who from earliest years has been telling us what the real world is'.[289]

In his Nobel Lecture Bellow ranged over many fascinating aspects of the development of the modern novel. Especially he was disappointed with the way so many critics had assumed that the notion of character was dead:

> The fact that the death notice of character 'has been signed by the most serious essays' means only that another group of mummies, the most respectable leaders of the intellectual community, has laid down the law. It amuses me that these serious essayists should be allowed to sign the death notices of literary forms. Should art follow culture? Something has gone wrong.

We should not, he believed, write in the ways presented to us by intellectuals: 'We must not make bosses of our intellectuals. And we do them no good by letting them run the arts. Should they, when they read novels, find nothing in them but the endorsement of their own opinions? Are we here on earth to play such games?' He firmly believed in art as a fount of insight, which was still preferred by many people to the alternatives on offer: 'Writers are greatly respected. The intelligent public is wonderfully patient with them, continues to read them and endures disappointment after disappointment, waiting to hear from art what it does not hear from theology, philosophy, social theory, and what it cannot hear from pure science.' And in a marvelously haunting turn of phrase he concluded with the opinion that the novel '…is a sort of latter-day lean-to, a hovel in which the spirit takes shelter'.[290]

In his Banquet Speech Bellow issued warnings, which should certainly give academics cause to be modest in their aims and would-be laureates to be modest in their expectations: 'For when I am praised on all sides I worry a bit…Universal agreement seems to open the door to dismissal. We know how often our contemporaries are mistaken. They are not invariably wrong, but it is not at all a bad idea to remember that they can't confer immortality on you.'[291]

The Threat of Mass Man

The award to Elias Canetti in 1981 clearly served to make known to a much wider audience the writings and ideas of an author who had been causing a stir among some intellectuals for quite some time. In an article in the British newspapre *The Sunday Times*, 18th October 1981, Salman Rushdie called him 'The Invisible Master' and 'the "Dr Who?" of our literary world'.

In his award ceremony speech Dr Johannes Edfelt described Canetti as an 'exiled and cosmopolitan author' who had 'one native land, and that is the German language'.[292] This is probably a good working identification for a man who was born in Bulgaria, lived in Britain, Ausria and Germany, finally taking on British citizenship, but living the last twenty years of his life mainly in Switzerland.

Edfelt stressed the qualities of two of Canetti's works, and one in particular, the novel which was translated as *Auto da Fé* (1935), but the original German title, *Die Blendung*, has various associations: the act of blinding, dazzling or deceiving. The other work was his study of *Crowds and Power* (1960).[293] The former is in many ways an imaginative embodiment of the insights expressed more systematically in the latter: the threat of the 'mass man' within all of us and the danger of extreme isolation of the individual brought about by the need for modern man to become specialized.

It is interesting to note that in his Banquet Speech Canetti devoted a large part of his time to expressing thanks to the four writers who had influenced him most, all of them writing in German, and none of them winners of the Nobel Prize: Karl Kraus, Franz Kafka, Robert Musil and Hermann Broch. His comment on Kafka provides incidentally an interesting way of interpreting Kafka's famous story *The Metamorphosis*: 'he was able to make himself small and thus escape the influence of power.'[294]

Not Magic but Real

The Columbian writer, Gabriel García Márquez [1982] has become closely identified with a unique combination of realism and fantasy, which has been exemplified in many works of Latin American writers, and has become known as 'magical realism'. Gyllensten, in his award ceremony speech, stressed that in García Márquez's novellas and short stories 'we are led into this peculiar place where the miraculous and the real converge'. At the beginning of his speech Gyllensten praised especially the novel *One Hundred Years of Solitude* (1967), which had been a huge international success. Since then he had confirmed his reputation with many other equally impressive novels. Like many other South American writers García Márquez was 'strongly committed politically on the side of the poor and the weak against oppression and economic exploitation'.[295]

In his Nobel Lecture, 'The Solitude of Latin America', García Márquez [1982] pointed out that the absurdities, myths and unexplained facts were actually part of the historical reality of South

America and not just the products of his own imagination. He cited some examples: the general who held a funeral for the loss of his right leg, and another general who invented a pendulum which he believed could detect poison in his food. There was also the case of the statue erected to yet another general, but which was in fact bought second hand from a warehouse in Paris and depicted someone else entirely. What Latin American writers lacked was not imagination but the means to express it convincingly: '…we have had to ask but little of imagination, for our crucial problem has been a lack of conventional means to render our lives believable. This, my friends, is the crux of our solitude.'[296] In the latter part of the lecture he reproached Europe for attempting to interpret and assess Latin America by using yardsticks appropriate only to their own cultures. It is this which has estranged South America even more, making it more remote from Europe, condemning it to the solitude of which he writes in his own work: 'The interpretation of our reality through patterns not our own, serves only to make us ever more unknown, ever less free, ever more solitary.'[297]

Living Another Life

In his award ceremony speech Lars Gyllensten explained how the works of the British author William Golding [1983] were effective on many levels. They had become world bestsellers because they were 'very entertaining and exciting' but they have also attracted scholars who have explored the ambiguities and complexities of his work. It is the combination of realistic detail and mythical significance that has made his works of universal interest. Gyllensten points out, in his final remarks directed at the laureate, that in interviews and essays Golding had made fun of attempts to fit his novels into a formula or pattern. Gyllensten added, 'That is impossible – simply because if it were possible there would be no reason for you to write your books…'[298]

There are echoes of some of the sentiments of Canetti concerning the individual and mass-man in Golding's Nobel Lecture, and reflections on the role the novel can play in preserving individuality:

Put simply the novel stands between us and the hardening concept of statistical man. There is no other medium in which we can live for so long and so intimately with a character. That is the service a novel renders. It performs no less an act than the rescue and the preservation of the individuality and dignity of the single being, be it man, woman or child. No other art, I claim, can so thread in and out of a single mind and body, so live another life.[299]

Going with the Flow

When the French novelist Claude Simon won the Nobel Prize in 1985, it was mainly as a representative of the style of the 'nouveau roman'. Gyllensten attempted to summarize the characteristics of the new style of writing in his award ceremony speech:

The new writers were against the more conventional fiction and broke its rules that a novel should have a realistic story and move along in a lucid and coherent way in time. Their prose works had the appearance of linguistic montages or collages. They took place in the dimensions of memory and the apparently arbitrary or free association.[300]

In his Nobel Lecture Simon deals dismissively with the accusations that had been made that the committee's selection had been influenced by the Russian secret service, the KGB (see also accounts of their supposed influence elsewhere in the present book). He deflates the accusations with irony: 'For indeed, the egoistic and vain gratuity of what some people call "art for art's sake" has been so reviled that it is no small recompense for me to see my writings, which have had no greater ambition than to raise themselves to that level, ranked among the instruments of revolutionary and upsetting action.'[301]

In the rest of his lecture Simon provided some stimulating thoughts on developments in the modern novel, with many witty asides along the way. For example, he cites one unnamed critic: 'Have they given Claude Simon the Nobel Prize to confirm the rumour that the novel is finally dead?' One important point he stresses is that the author is never completely in control of what he is producing. It is not a matter of creating something from a predetermined formula:

And immediately I find that, first: what one writes (or describes) is never something which has happened prior to the work of writing. On the contrary it produces itself (in every sense of the term) in the course of working, within its own *present*. It is the upshot, not of the conflict between the very vague initial project and the language, but, on the contrary, of their symbiosis, so that, at least in my case, the result is infinitely richer than the intention.[302]

Late Arrival

The Egyptian Naguib Mahfouz [1988] was given the award for his major contribution to the development of the novel in Arabic literature. In the words of Sture Allén in his award ceremony speech, 'In Arabic literature, the novel is actually a twentieth century phenomenon, more or less contemporary with Mahfouz. And it was he who, in due course, was to bring it to maturity.'[303] It is ironic therefore that, according to Mahfouz himself in his Nobel Lecture, many people did not even know who he was: 'I was told by a foreign correspondent in Cairo that the moment my name was mentioned in connection with the prize silence fell, and many wondered who I was.' Mahfouz went on to talk of the problems of the Third World and finally he apologized for disturbing the peace of the Nobel ceremony. Quite consciously and deliberately he was using the occasion as a platform for his ideas on the plights of the Third World:

> …I feel I may have somewhat troubled your calm. But what do you expect from one coming from the Third World? Is not every vessel coloured by what it contains? Besides, where can the moans of Mankind find a place to resound if not in your oasis of civilization planted by its great founder for the service of science, literature and sublime human values.[304]

Oppression on Two Continents

It is interesting to note that when Sture Allén made his award ceremony speech for the South African writer Nadine Gordimer in 1991, his emphasis was mainly on the political content of her work rather than on any stylistic aspects. Structure, form and the general concept of a novel are not mentioned: 'she makes visible the extremely complicated and utterly inhuman living conditions in the world of racial segregation. She feels political responsibility, and does not shy away from its consequences…'[305]

There are many perceptive and stimulating thoughts in Gordimer's Nobel Lecture. Perhaps the most encouraging idea for other writers is that one should write without worrying what others will think, but nevertheless in the hope that you will find some enthusiastic readers. One should avoid '…the temptations, conscious and unconscious, which lure the writer into keeping a corner of the eye on who will take offence, who will approve what is on the page – a temptation that, like Eurydice's straying glance, will lead the writer back into the Shades of a destroyed talent.'[306]

In the case of the Afro-American writer Toni Morrison [1993], Allén, in his award ceremony speech, while providing some thoughts on her depiction of the Afro-American lifestyle, focused more on her original and imaginative style: 'The reader derives vast pleasure from her superb narrative technique, shifting from novel to novel and marked by original development, although it is related to Faulkner and to the Latin American tradition. Toni Morrison's novels invite the reader to partake at many levels, and at varying degrees of complexity.'[307]

Allén mentioned three novels, and it is clear that the then latest, *Jazz*, impressed the committee especially. Not only is the novel about the lives of a number of people in 'the jazz age' in Harlem in the 1920s, but her 'approach is similar to the style in which jazz is performed'. He provided some impression of this technique: 'In the course of the novel we perceive a first-person narrator, varying, supplementing and intensifying the story. The final picture is a highly composite image of events, characters and atmospheres, mediated in sensual language with a deep inherent sense of musicality.'[308]

In one part of her Nobel Lecture Morrison focuses on the various ways language is used to oppress. She lists the many types of abuse that are incorporated in language: 'obscuring state language', 'faux-language of mindless media', 'calcified language of the academy' and many other manifestations of such abuse. For her such language abuse must be 'rejected, altered and exposed'. And in words which echoed the sentiments of Foucault she talked of 'the policing languages of mastery' which do not permit new knowledge.[309]

Writing as Exorcism

In 1994 Japan had its second literary laureate: Kenzaburō Ōe. Here again it was the technical aspects of Ōe's writing which came in for particular praise. The focus was on his qualities as an experimental writer. In the novel *The Silent Cry* (1967) he blended two different time frames simultaneously, and his subsequent novels reveal close connections with each other and are clearly variations of each other, to such an extent that, as Espmark remarked (he gave the award ceremony speech on that occasion), Ōe is 'a writer not writing books but "building" an *oeuvre*'. According to Espmark in his speech, Ōe claims he has not sought a worldwide audience but speaks only to Japanese people, and that his writing clearly has a predominantly therapeutic function for him: 'Ōe has described his writing as a way of exorcising his demons.'[310] But he did not explain what these demons were.

But if this makes Ōe's art seem to be akin to art therapy, then Ōe himself revealed in his Nobel Lecture that he nevertheless used the persona to gain access to the world: '...the fundamental style of my writing has been to start from my personal matters and then to link it up with society, the state and the world'.[311]

The Human Menagery

The award ceremony speech by Horace Engdahl for Günter Grass makes it sound at times as though the prize is a kind of lifetime achievement award but also testifies to Grass' continuing experimental approach to writing. Since the publication of *The Tin Drum* (1959), in Engdahl's words, he was reproached for the fact 'that, after being so loved by readers and critics, he had the audacity to write...differently.' Grass treated recent European history, German history in particular, not as tragedy but as farce. He criticized through mockery: 'This was an achievement far more radical than all the ideological criticism directed against Nazism.' He revealed the baseness in man, 'bringing human forms close to the animal world'. Hence 'his menagerie of cat and mouse, dog, snail, flounder, frog and scarecrow'.[312] Again and again in his works Grass has compared individual characters to specific animals in order to explore certain personality traits though grotesque exaggeration.

His Nobel Lecture included broad-ranging reflections on storytelling, literature and politics, capitalism and the economy, Grass also attempted to answer the question 'What made you become a writer?' His answer was that it was essentially a desire to blend the realm of the imagination with politics:

> The ability to daydream at length, the job of punning and playing with language in general, the addiction to lying for its own sake rather than for mine because sticking to the truth would have been a bore – in short, what is loosely known as talent was certainly a factor, but it was the abrupt intrusion of politics into the family idyll that turned the all too flighty category of talent into a ballast with a certain permanence and depth.[313]

A Genre Unto Himself

The main point to arise from Engdahl's reflections on the British writer, V.S. Naipaul [2001], in his award ceremony speech is that he is a writer impossible to categorize in terms of traditional genre. He developed in fact a unique genre, which is best described simply as 'prose in the style of Naipaul'. If one were to try and characterize his style, argued Engdahl, it would have to be by omission rather than by definition, for it is the innocent wide-eyed view of the child which is his ideal, avoiding all flourishes and 'expressive hyperbole'.[314]

In his Nobel Lecture, 'Two Worlds', Naipaul stressed that what had been crucial in his life as a writer was reliance on intuition. Abstraction and analysis would have yielded nothing: 'Whatever extra there is in me at any given moment isn't fully formed. I am hardly aware of it; it awaits the next book. It will – with luck – come to me during the actual writing, and it will take me by surprise. That element of surprise is what I look for when I am writing.' It is a firm lesson to those writers who consider working out elaborate plans and plots before they write:

I have trusted to intuition. I did it at the beginning. I do it even now. I have no idea how things might turn out, where in my writing I might go next. I have trusted to my intuition to find the subjects, and I have written intuitively. I have an idea when I start, I have a shape; but I will fully understand what I have written only after some years.

One can perceive here parallels with Ōe: 'Each book, intuitively sensed and, in the case of fiction, intuitively worked out, stands on what has gone before, and grows out of it. I feel that at any stage of my literary career it could have been said that the last book contained all the others.' He reiterates this credo nearer the end of his lecture: 'I said I was an intuitive writer. That was so, and that remains so now, when I am nearly at the end. I never had a plan. I followed no system. I worked intuitively. My aim every time was to do a book, to create something that would be easy and interesting to read.' If he had attempted to analyse in an abstract way he felt sure that he would never have been able to write: 'I had never used abstract words to describe any writing purpose of mine. If I had, I would never have been able to do the book. The book was done intuitively, and only out of close observation.'[315]

Lending Voice to the Despised

In Per Wästberg's comments (in his award ceremony speech) on the novel *Disgrace* (1999) by the South African writer, J.M. Coetzee [2003], he outlines the themes which characterize all his writing: 'race and gender, ownership and violence, and the moral and political complicity of everyone in that borderland where the languages of liberation and reconciliation carry no meaning'. In his introduction he had summarized these themes much more succinctly: 'Coetzee sees through the obscene poses and false pomp of history, lending voice to the silenced and the despised.'[316]

In his Banquet Speech Coetzee said that his main regret was that he would not be able to tell his deceased mother about the prize; for his Nobel Lecture he preferred to read a complex metaphorical tale.

The Force that Bends to Nothing

There has already been some account earlier in the present book about the obscurity of the writing of Elfriede Jelinek and when one considers what she can teach the aspiring laureate, it has to be admitted that while obscurity may persuade judges of the profundity of a writer's work, it is not a promising characteristic for lesser mortals to adopt. In Jelinek's case more clarity can be obtained from Engdahl's award ceremony speech than from her Nobel Lecture. At the end of his speech he does not mince his words, and refers to the difficulties in her writing when addressing words directly to her: 'If literature by definition is a force that bends to nothing, you are in our day one of its truest representatives.'[317]

One should also bear in mind the BBC report on 11th October 2005, in which it was announced that Knut Ahnlund, a member of the Swedish Academy, had stepped down because of the 2004 award to Jelinek. In the newspaper *Svenska Dagbladet* Ahnlund wrote: 'Last year's Nobel Prize has not only done irreparable damage to all progressive forces, it has also confused the general view of literature as an art... After this, I cannot even formally remain in the Swedish Academy. As of now, I consider myself an outsider.' He also expressed doubts as to whether the Academy members had actually read very much of Jelinek's work.[318]

It has not been explained why Ahnlund had waited a whole year till just before the announcement of the 2005 winner to make his feelings public. Had he just discovered that he could also make neither head nor tail of the works by that year's winner, Harold Pinter, and felt that enough was enough?

The Second Being

For the laureate Orhan Pamuk [2006] there were to be serious and problematic consequences to his award, but in this context of reflections on the vicissitudes of the modern novel, it is useful to consider first the circumstances of the award itself and the reasons for it, and not blur the picture with other issues.

Engdahl, in his award ceremony speech, made it clear that Pamuk is a writer who is not only concerned with investigating the complexity of his native land, Turkey, and its problems, but also explored the relationship between traditional Muslim culture and the industrialization of the West. In his choice of the novel genre he is consciously allowing both cultures to interact. In Engdahl's words 'He had to be both Easterner – to understand what he was seeing – and Westerner to have the method to portray it.'[319]

Engdahl focused on three of his works. *My Name is Red* (1998) tells of a sixteenth century artist and reflects the different views of the individual in Eastern and Western art. *The Black Book* (1990) takes a fantastic journey through night-time Istanbul, and focuses on how people escape from themselves by fleeing into unreal lives: 'civilization appears as a boundless plagiarism'.[320] In *Snow* (2002) a poet influenced by western culture surveys Turkish society from a remote town.

In his Banquet Speech Pamuk suggested various personal answers to the question 'Why do you write?' The answer which is the most convincing for him is that it is to maintain the child's perspective on the world: 'Literature is about happiness, I wanted to say, about preserving your childishness all your life, keeping the child in you alive...'[321]

The political furore that arose around Pamuk and caused his name to hit the international headlines had nothing essentially to do with the Nobel Prize. From one perspective the accusations against him had nothing to do with the fact that he was a writer; but from another they have everything to do with it. The bare facts of the case are as follows. In February 2005, he gave an interview to a Swiss newspaper, the *Tages-Anzeiger*, and it was also published in other newspapers. In this he said: 'Thirty thousand Kurds and one million Armenians were killed in these lands, and nobody but me dares talk about it.' In June of that year Turkey introduced a new penal code including Article 301, which states that 'A person who being a Turk, explicitly insults the republic or Turkish Grand National Assembly, shall be punishable by imprisonment of between six months and three years.' The clause was applied retroactively and Pamuk was charged with violating it. In October, after the trial had begun, he reiterated the views he had expressed in the Swiss newspaper. Turkish law required that the prosecution of Pamuk should be approved by the Ministry of Justice. Just after the trial started on 16th December, the judge ruled that approval had not been received and suspended proceedings. On 22nd January 2006, the Ministry of Justice refused to issue an approval of the prosecution, saying they had no authority within the new penal code. The next day it was ruled that the trial could not continue. The charges were dropped.

Thus essentially it was a legal dispute but also, because Pamuk was one of Turkey's most prominent writers, it became an issue of freedom of expression. Pamuk confirmed this view himself in an interview in the BBC World 'Hardtalk' series in April 2006.

There was an international outcry at the case, not least because Turkey was under consideration for membership of the European Union, a point that the BBC emphasized in its reporting. Many MEPs felt that it was unacceptable for Turkey to become a member, while it still restrained free speech in such a fashion. The International PEN Club and Amnesty International also did their best to whip up international opinion against Turkey.[322]

Perhaps of greater concern to the would-be laureate than the free-speech issue is the fact that Pamuk has also been accused of plagiarism. He was accused by another Turkish author in a national Turkish newspaper (*Hürriyet*). And another accusation was brought that his novel *The White Castle* (1985) contained paragraphs lifted word for word from a novel by Fuad Carim (*Istanbul in the Time of the Kanuni*). Pamuk has refused to answer questions on these matters however. A favourable interpretation of the similarities can be found in Pamuk's postmodern literary style and as such they should not be referred to as plagiarism but as an example of intertextuality.[323]

His Nobel Lecture, 'My Father's Suitcase', takes its cue from an occasion when his father left him a suitcase to be opened after his death and containing his own manuscripts and literary efforts. Amongst other reflections, Pamuk provided insights in the lecture into the state of mind of a writer: 'A writer is someone who spends years patiently trying to discover the second being inside him, and the world that makes him who he is: when I speak of writing, what comes first to mind is not a novel, a poem, or literary tradition, it is a person who shuts himself up in a room, sits down at a table, and alone, turns inward; amid its shadows, he builds a new world with words.' He also echoed other writers who were concerned about provincialism, feeling that at some times in his life he had been 'marooned in the provinces' and one finds echoes of Böll in his words a little later: '…the greatest dilemmas facing humanity are still landlessness, homelessness, and hunger…'[324]

That Empty Space

It is very clear from Per Wästberg's award ceremony speech introducing the British writer Doris Lessing [2007] that a life's work was being rewarded. He was unequivocal in his closing words: 'Your lifework and your great pioneering effort are today not fulfilled but crowned with a prize you have long deserved.' He managed to present a broad panorama of her accomplishments in a brief span of time. All the major social, political and cultural issues of the twentieth century were covered in her works, from feminism, environmental issues and prejudice, to corruption, the homeless and tyranny. Interestingly, from the point of view of would-be laureates, while most of her major works can be referred to as novels, they also defy categorization in traditional senses. Wästberg said 'We stroll through the great library of her work, where all sections are unmarked and all genre classifications pointless.'[325]

Lessing's Nobel Lecture, 'On not winning the Nobel Prize', provides a stimulating assessment of the importance of books, those things with covers and printed pages, not the electronic transference of words which has nowadays appropriated the word 'book', prefixing it with an 'e'. She made a spirited attack on the mindlessness of blogging: '…this internet, which has seduced a whole generation with its inanities so that even quite reasonable people will confess that once they are hooked, it is hard to cut free, and they may find a whole day has passed in blogging etc.'[326]

For the writer, she argued, it is crucial to be connected to the great tradition of writing that has gone before. A writer cannot exist in isolation from the writings of others. Checking the speeches of recent laureates she had found that Pamuk's father had had 500 books, Naipaul had spent much time in the British Library and Coetzee 'was not only close to the great tradition, he was the tradition: he taught literature in Cape Town'.[327]

Thus she concluded: 'In order to write, in order to make literature, there must be a close connection with libraries, books, with the Tradition.' Also necessary for all writers, she claims, is finding 'that empty space which should surround you when you write'. This sounds similar not only to the view of Virginia Woolf, but also to Pamuk's emphasis on the writer's need to shut himself or herself away in a room. Lessing asserted that much publicized and feted new writers often lose that space where their creativity flourished. Older, mature, established writers know how crucial this space is: 'And we, the old ones, want to whisper into those innocent ears. "Have you still got your space? Your soul, your own and necessary place where your own voices may speak to you, you alone, where you may dream. Oh, hold onto it, don't let it go.'"[328]

Writers and critics have hastened to label many Nobel awards as political in nature, and this is primarily because connections can be so easily be drawn between a writer's ideas and commitments and the current state of the world. But these claims are usually expressed in the form of surmises: hard evidence is difficult to come by. Thus in an article in *The Nation*, by Dan Kellum, on the occasion of the award to Lessing, it was claimed 'For better or worse, Ms Lessing's selection, then, is absolutely in keeping with the political imperatives that seem to underlie the Swedish Academy's agenda.' If one is to judge by Wästberg's words however Lessing was regarded as political only in the broadest sense and not as a supporter of any particular ideology: 'She has revealed the totalitarian temptations and shown us the strength of undogmatic humanism.'[329]

The Groping Writer

Jean-Marie Gustave Le Clézio, the 2008 laureate, was praised by Horace Engdahl for his breaking down of traditional genre distinctions. In this way Le Clézio was continuing the ideals of the French *nouveau roman*. In his second book, *Fever* (1965), he had written 'Poems, short stories and novels are antiquities that no longer fool anyone or just about… All that is left is the writing, writing, writing that gropes its way along…'[330] Le Clézio's writing was greatly affected by his travels. He spent several years, for example, in Central America, tracing his own ancestors' migrations. These experiences of other cultures greatly affected his view of European civilization. Of his novel *Desert* (1980) Engdahl said, 'The open form of this book has become typical for its author, a form that juxtaposes separate places, times, and discourses without mediation. In his hands the novel merges with the travel story, the analytical essay, the prose of recollection, and witness literature.'[331]

It becomes clear that Le Clézio was being rewarded for his universalism: '…you are yourself a nomad of the world' and a little later Engdahl added 'You have…restored to literature its power to celebrate the world.'[332]

In Le Clézio's Nobel Lecture there are echoes of Doris Lessing's sentiments concerning the crucial role he allocates to books in his development: 'For want of any children's books, I read my grandmother's dictionaries. They were like a marvellous gateway, through which I embarked on a discovery of the world, to wander and daydream as I looked at the illustrated plates, and the maps, and the lists of unfamiliar words.' The books in his father's library became the source of his wonderment at the world: 'It was then that I understood a truth not immediately apparent to children, that books are a treasure more precious than any real property or bank account. It was in those volumes – most of them ancient, bound tomes – that I discovered the great works of world literature…' But the books which had the greatest impact on him were the anthologies of traveller's tales: '…those books gave me a taste for adventure, gave me a sense of the vastness of the real world, a means to explore it through instinct and the senses rather than through knowledge.'[333]

Life Under the Boot

The German writer Herta Müller [2009] also owes her birth as a writer to books. In her Banquet Speech she told how she attended the preparatory school against her mother's will: 'She knew that if I moved to the city I would become corrupted. And I was. I started to read books.'[33] Growing up under the dictatorship of Ceauşescu in Romania, she learned to use language to express her opposition. In some ways the focus of her work is narrow, as indicated by Ander Olsson in his award ceremony speech: 'Almost everything she writes is about life under Ceauşescu's Romanian dictatorship, its fear and betrayal and constant surveillance.'[33] But this has become a way of protesting against totalitarianism in general. In her Banquet Speech Müller reminded her listeners of this:

> …to this very day there are dictatorships of every stripe. Some go on forever, always frightening us anew, such as Iran. Others, such as Russia and China, don cloaks of respectability; they liberalize their economies, but human rights remain firmly in the grip of Stalinism or Maoism. And then there are the half-democracies of Eastern Europe, which since 1989 have been putting on and taking off their respectable cloaks so often that they're practically in tatters.

But literature can preserve and advocate the value of the individual, and it was in this spirit that she concluded her Banquet Speech: 'Literature speaks with everyone individually – it is personal property that stays inside our heads. And nothing speaks to us as forcefully as a book, which expects nothing in return, other than that we think and feel.'[336]

On a personal note, the present author can report that Herta Müller is the only winner of the Nobel Prize in Literature that he has knowingly come in close proximity to (after a reading at the Goethe Institut, Seoul). And he can confirm that she is not very tall, likes a glass of wine and becomes very annoyed if her reading is interrupted by a mobile phone and if, in subsequent discussion, she is asked intrusive personal questions.

Writing as Refuge

The Peruvian writer Mario Vargas Llosa [2010] is a protester against tyranny and one who employs all literary genres, but was rewarded primarily for his novels. Wästberg, in his award ceremony speech, commented that he was hard to classify: he is 'a citizen of the world, a Marxist transformed by Castro's misdeeds into a liberal, a losing presidential candidate later to appear on his country's postage stamps, an epic poet and historian, a satirist,

an eroticist, an essayist and columnist...' Wästberg argues that for Vargas Llosa literature is a way of defending the rights of the individual: 'Vargas Llosa believes in the force of literature. Without literature there would be no rendition of mankind's possibilities and hidden places.'[337]

In his Nobel Lecture, 'In Praise of Reading and Fiction', Vargas Llosa reveals that he is yet another laureate for whom learning to read books was a key moment in his development: 'I learned to read at the age of five... It is the most important thing that has ever happened to me.' Then through literature he related to and interpreted the world: 'reading changed dreams into life and life into dreams and placed the universe of literature within reach of the boy I once was. My mother told me the first things I wrote were continuations of the stories I read because it made me sad when they concluded or because I wanted to change their endings.' Writing as a refuge was also important for him: 'I have been able to devote most of my time to the passion, the vice, the marvel of writing, creating a parallel life where we can take refuge against adversity, one that makes the extraordinary natural and the natural extraordinary, that dissipates chaos, beautifies ugliness, eternalizes the moment, and turns death into a passing spectacle.'[338]

There is much indeed that can be gleaned from his lecture, much that supports the argument for the importance of literature in life. Let one passage on the civilizing role of literature suffice to suggest the spirit of the whole:

> ...civilization is now less cruel than when storytellers began to humanize life with their fables. We would be worse than we are without the good books we have read, more conformist,

not as restless, more submissive, and the critical spirit, the engine of progress, would not even exist. Like writing, reading is a protest against the insufficiencies of life.[339]

Getting Your Act Together

There are a few more disparate aspects of the history of the Nobel Prize in Literature which are worth considering before entertaining serious hopes of success. There are, for example, some maverick laureates worth reflecting on. And if you are of a comic bent, attention should be paid to the one true comic talent to win the prize. Should you also, in the light of all that we have pondered together, modify your style to please theorists and critics? And what of all those great writers who were nominated but never selected, not to mention the ones who won but have been consigned to oblivion? Finally if your case seems truly hopeless, are there any other options worth considering to ensure your lasting fame as a writer?

A Class of Their Own

The Bellicose Neutral, or Praising with Faint Damnation
There have been some laureates who somehow do not fit into any of the observable trends, and have proved therefore to have been unique phenomena. One such writer is the Swiss, Carl Spitteler (awarded in 1920 for 1919). Although he had attracted attention with one work in particular, even at the time he had many detractors. At this distance in time it is difficult to imagine what all the fuss was about, and it is even more difficult to find

anyone who has read any of his works either in the original German or in translation.

He was born in Liestal in 1845, studied law in Zurich and theology both in Zurich and Heidelberg. He spent some time as a private tutor in St Petersberg and as an elementary school teacher in Switzerland. He also worked as an editor for the *Neue Zürcher Zeitung*.

Apart from various prose works, the work for which he became especially well known was an epic allegorical poem in iambic pentameters called *Olympic Spring*, written in the period 1900 to 1905 and published in 1906. Looking back on the time when it was first published, he wrote in the 'Autobiography' he supplied for the Nobel Committee: 'The first two parts remained as unnoticed as all my other books.'[340]

Espmark's account of the fortunes of Spitteler's nomination does not make inspiring reading.[341] Already in 1912 he was being considered for a split prize. In 1913 he was considered for the prize, but the committee was looking to break with the tradition established since the prize's inception.[342] At the outbreak of war in 1914 Spitteler suddenly became the 'unanimously proposed choice'. He was praised as the 'voice of neutrality' and for being 'above the contradictions of the age'.[343] In 1915 the committee considered him for the 'reserved' 1914 prize, but then he blotted his copybook: he started to express openly his opposition to the pro-German attitude of the Swiss-German-speaking minority in Switzerland, especially in an essay 'Our Swiss Point of View'. This led the Nobel Committee into the dangerous waters of becoming concerned about upsetting the Germans and the Austrians with their choice. There was criticism of Spitteler's 'bellicose polemics' which might 'cause the utmost embarrassment and instigate manifold misinterpretations'.[344]

By 1919 concern about Spitteler's political utterances had died down, but due to the war the number of nominations was low, so that the committee had few candidates to choose between.[345] They made use therefore of their right to propose candidates themselves to bump up the numbers. Concerning Spitteler however strong criticism came from committee member Henrik Schück who felt that the author's fame could only be explained 'by confusing, as so often happens in Germany, *intention* and artistic *capacity*, the idea and the execution'.[346] One cannot help but notice the bitter nationalistic sentiment here which is to some degree understandable so shortly after the horrors of the First World War. In the end, the prizes for 1918 and 1919 were suspended again, and the 1919 prize was awarded to Spitteler in 1920.

Hjärne's comments in his Presentation Speech, in which he attempted to stress Spitteler's unique achievement with his main poetic work, *Olympic Spring*, also reveal the reservations which the committee had about him. A summary of his main points makes it clear that there were many characteristics of Spitteler's writing which did not work in his favour. Hjärne spoke of his 'merits not immediately obvious', his being 'out of step with the times', his choice of subject 'bound to bewilder and even repel', 'his choice of an idiosyncratic mythology' and 'wilful abuse of mythological names'. Finally he used deliberate and often jarring anachronisms. Referring to the storyline of the poem Hjärne spoke of 'the plot of the impudent flatfoot people to deprive Apollo of his universal rule by means of an artificial sun and their overweening attempt to attack him in the air by means of a treacherously constructed vehicle and poison gas…'[347] In Spitteler's favour it must be said that this makes him appear to have been remarkably prescient when he wrote the work in the early 1900s.

If Spitteler is little read nowadays he was influential in his day. Sigmund Freud named one of his psychoanalytical periodicals after Spitteler's novel *Imago* of 1906, and also borrowed a convention he found in this novel. The character called Viktor had the habit of calling his body 'Konrad', as though it were a friend, because he felt he got along with it very well. The name 'Konrad' became a catchphrase for Freud and his circle which they frequently used when talking about 'the human body' (as in a letter to Karl Abraham, 21st July 1925). Carl Jung is also known to have been interested in the symbolic and mythological aspects of Spitteler's works (evidence is provided by the many references to the author in Jung's book, *Psychological Types*).

The Literary Laureate Who Never Was

Buttonhole someone indiscriminately at a cocktail party with the question 'Which Nobel Prize did Churchill win?' and you are quite likely to receive the answer 'Well, it must have been the Peace Prize, I suppose.' Those readers who have stayed with the present book this far, and have managed to pay close attention, will know that the correct answer should have been, 'The Nobel Prize in Literature, of course.' Here's another one to spring on unsuspecting friends: 'Which Nobel Prize did the famous German writer Carl von Ossietzky win?' Having loaded your question sufficiently in that way, the response is likely to be 'For literature, one assumes' (do not of course expect your friend to be familiar with the niceties of prepositional usage in the Swedish Academy). In other times and under other political circumstances, he might have been proposed for it of course. Contemporaries compared his satirical work to that of Voltaire and Heinrich Heine, and his literary style was greatly praised by other highly respected writers, such as Arnold Zweig and Kurt Tucholsky. Fate would have it however that he was a pacifist in Hitler's Germany. The answer to the second question should thus be, 'The Nobel Peace Prize, of course.' The Nobel Peace Prize was not awarded in 1935: the award was postponed and given to Ossietzky in 1936.

Carl von Ossietzky was born in Hamburg, Germany. Seven years after his father died in 1891 his mother married a Social Democrat called Gustav Walther, who was very influential in shaping Ossietzky's political views. After the First World War he became a confirmed pacifist, made many public speeches in

Hamburg in which he endeavoured to persuade people to adopt a philosophy of peace and became president of the local chapter of the German Peace Society, later moving to the organization's headquarters in Berlin. After working as a journalist for several publications, he finally took over the editorship of the periodical *Die Weltbühne* in 1926, continuing the policy of publicizing the secret rearmament of Germany. As a result of this he was tried for libel and betraying military secrets and spent several periods in prison. On 28th February 1933, the morning after the Reichstag fire he was arrested, imprisoned and eventually sent to a concentration camp.

When he was awarded the Nobel Peace Prize, the German press was forbidden to comment on it and he was prevented from travelling to Norway to accept it. Hitler subsequently ordered that no German citizen should accept a Nobel Prize of any kind, and set up a special German National Prize as some kind of consolation in 1937. Ossietzky was kept under constant surveillance in hospital till he died in 1938 of the after-effects of tuberculosis and maltreatment in the concentration camps.

In his award ceremony speech in 1936 Fredrik Stang, then chairman of the Nobel Committee for the Peace Prize also made a point of praising Ossietzky's literary qualities: 'The role in which he is best known, however, is that of journalist and essayist. He is an author of note; his style is supple, elegant, often bitingly witty.'[348]

There is an object lesson in all this, justifying this brief aside on the Peace Prize, for all would-be literary laureates: if a campaign in supporting you for the prize in literature is obviously getting you nowhere, try a little harder to pursue in a very public way some humanitarian ideals, such as working vociferously for world peace. Someone may propose you for the Nobel Peace Prize, which is quite a decent consolation prize. Just try not to get yourself incarcerated before the date of the award ceremony.

Laugh? I Could Have Cried! or
The Black Man, the Jew and the Clown

To what extent can you maintain hopes of being awarded the Nobel Prize in Literature if your primary aim is to make people laugh? Many writers have incorporated some comedy and wit into their works but primarily as a device for certain intellectual ends, to change ways of thinking, to promote political or social ideals, etc. George Bernard Shaw and Günter Grass spring to mind immediately and there are others who have preferred the subtle use of irony, such as Thomas Mann. For few however has it been their guiding principle and priority, while reflecting a social conscience, to make their readers, or audiences, laugh uproariously. Only one of the laureates stands out in this respect: Dario Fo. This provides a stark warning to would-be laureates in the field of comedy: the odds are stacked against you.

In his award ceremony speech Sture Allén attempted to provide some account of the artistry in comedy: 'To be a jester is, and always has been, a serious matter.' Comedy is an effective method of expressing unpleasant truths: 'Mixing laughter and seriousness is his way of telling the truth about abuses and unrighteousness.'[349]

Fo's Nobel Lecture is full of the tongue-in-cheek provocative statements that have made him so successful as a dramatist. By awarding the prize to a jester, he asked his audience, have the Swedish Academy finally gone too far: 'But, dear members of the Academy, let's admit it, this time you've overdone it. I mean come on, first you give the prize to a black man, then to a Jewish writer. Now you give it to a clown. What gives?'

Up to the Mark?

An Explosive Style

It was inevitable that some writers, in their Banquet Speeches or Lectures, or both, would not be able to resist alluding to the fact that the great man, in whose name the prize was being awarded to them, also, apart from being concerned to encourage peace in the world and the advancement of science and literary excellence, happened to be the inventor of dynamite. This fact should lend courage to those would-be laureates who might feel somewhat anxious about their style and content being in any way explosive!

William Faulkner [1949] was of course thinking of the atomic bomb, when he made his remarks in his Banquet Speech, but his implication was that the advances in methods of destructive warfare had been so extensive as to make everybody's primary concern that of survival. If, in the twenty-first century, we no longer talk so much about the dangers of the atomic bomb, there is still the perennial concern about the explosive devices of terrorists. For Faulkner this concern for survival worked against what he considered the true realm and focus of literature: the human heart. Such an idea would seem to echo Nobel's own concerns: having discovered how to destroy, he wanted to reward those who created. Faulkner said:

> Our tragedy today is a general and universal physical fear so long sustained by now that we can even bear it. There are no longer problems of the spirit. There is only the question: When will I be blown up? Because of this, the young man or woman writing today has forgotten the problems of the human heart in conflict with itself which alone can make good writing because only that is worth writing about, worth the agony and the sweat.[350]

Near the end of his Nobel Lecture, Heinrich Böll argued that literature has always been involved in a process of changing its forms: 'It is not merely for frivolity nor only to shock that art and literature have again and again transformed their forms, discovering new ones by experiment.' In terms of contents too the arts have always endeavoured to present something new 'and that something was almost never the confirmation of what existed and was already available'. Art itself was like a bomb, full of explosive ideas: 'Art is always a good hiding-place, not for dynamite, but for intellectual explosives and social time bombs.'[351]

In his Banquet Speech in 1967, Miguel Ángel Asturias, took up the theme of the close relationship between destructive and creative forces. He referred to Nobel's character as 'that dreamer who with the passing of time would shock the world with his inventions – the discovery of the most destructive explosives then known – for helping man in his titanic chores of mining, digging tunnels, and constructing roads and canals.' Nobel's dreams, he maintained, made possible the great achievements of establishing civilization in the Americas. South American novels also, he said, aimed to destroy original structures to make way for the new:

> ...the secret mines of the people, buried under tons of mis-understanding, prejudices, and taboos, bring to light in our narrative – between fable and myths – with blows of protest, testimony, and denouncement, dikes of letters which, like sands, contain reality to let the dream flow free or, on the contrary, contain the dream to let reality escape.[352]

In consideration of the dramatists who have won the Nobel Prize, mention has already been made of Wole Soyinka's identification of Nobel with an African god. Here the emphasis can be repeated, because that deity, Ogun, as Soyinka explained in his Banquet Speech in 1986, was the god of both destruction and creativity. The aim of that deity was to blast a route to enable the gods to be reunited with man: 'This deity anticipated your scientist Alfred Nobel at the beginning of time by clearing a path through primordial chaos, dynamiting his way through the core of earth to open a route for his fellow deities who sought to be reunited with us, mortals.'[353]

For Günter Grass, Nobel's invention has both positive and negative potential, which he called, in his Nobel Lecture, 'weal and woe': 'Just as the Nobel Prize – once we divest it of its ceremonial garb – has its roots in the invention of dynamite, which like such other human headbirths as the splitting of the atom and the likewise Nobelified classification of the gene has wrought both weal and woe in the world...' Thus also, he argued, literature destroys for the sake of creating the new: '...so literature has an explosive quality at its root, though the explosions literature releases have a delayed-action effect and change the world only in the magnifying glass of time, so to speak, it too wreaking cause for both joy and lamentation here below.'[354]

The challenge for Grass was to maintain literary quality while being subversive: 'How can subversive writing be both dynamite and of literary quality?' He also expressed scepticism about the ability of the internet to really stimulate creativity of good quality. Rather it dissipates creative energy: 'Is it not rather the case that literature is currently retreating from public life and that young writers are using the internet as a playground? A standstill, to which the suspicious word "communication" lends a certain aura, is making headway.'[355]

Attitudes to Theory, or Crossing the Tightrope

One question that occurs to all writers at some time, and especially if they dream of gaining international critical acclaim, is: to what extent should I take into account all this critical theory flying around about literature? Do I really have to provide some sort of evidence of familiarity with, let alone understanding of, all those schools of thought that have proliferated throughout the twentieth century and haunt us still in the twenty-first? As I write do I have to constantly bear in mind structuralist and poststructuralist perspectives, modernist and post-modern features, how the text might be deconstructed, whether females would take offence, what its eco-critical aspects are, and all those 'isms' that come and go like fads on a catwalk? And should one really heed what critics, scholars and popular journalists say?

It seems that one can learn much concerning theory and practice from the history of the Chinese novel, according to Pearl Buck in her Nobel Lecture: 'For the novelist believed that he should not be conscious of techniques. He should write as the material demanded. If a novelist became known for a particular style or technique, to that extent he ceased to be a good novelist and became a literary technician.'[356]

It has been noticed already in consideration of Pearl Buck as a novelist that she distinguished between the 'primary process' of actual creation and the 'secondary process' of analysis. As soon as the author becomes preoccupied with the 'secondary process' he, or she, is doomed as a writer. Only the ordinary people who are not concerned about what constitutes art can, paradoxically, judge the quality of a work of art: 'These are the ones who can really judge the work of the novelist, for they judge by that single test of reality. And the standard of the test is not to be made by the device of art, but by the single comparison of the reality of what they read, to their own reality.'[357]

It should be recalled that Saul Bellow [1976] (in the section on the novel in this book) urged writers not to regard intellectuals as their 'bosses' and William Golding [1983] warned by implication against too much respect for statistics. He did not use the concept 'sociology' but he was essentially distinguishing between writing a novel and practising that discipline: 'Put simply the novel stands between us and the hardening concept of statistical man. There is no other medium in which we can live for so long and so intimately with a character. That is the service a novel renders. It performs no less an act than the rescue and the preservation of the individuality and dignity of the single being, be it man, woman or child.'[358]

Octavio Paz [1990], in his Nobel Lecture, 'In Search of the Present', questioned the very vocabulary of critical theory. For example he asked: 'What is modernity? First of all it is an ambiguous term: there are as many types of modernity as there are societies. Each has its own. The word's meaning is uncertain and arbitrary…' And the concept of 'post-modernity' is also undermined: 'Modernity has been a universal passion. Since 1850 she has been our goddess and our demoness. In recent years, there has been an attempt to exorcise her and there has been much talk of "postmodernism". But what is postmodernism if not an even more modern modernity?'[359]

For Nadine Gordimer in her Nobel Lecture, 'Writing and Being', all critical theory only aims to pin down analytically something which is essentially intuitive: 'Yet from what is regarded as old-hat psychological analysis to modernism and post-modernism, structuralism and poststructuralism, all literary studies are aimed at the same end: to pin down to a consistency (and what is consistency if not the principle hidden within the riddle?); to make definitive through methodology the writer's grasp at the forces of being.' She cited Roland Barthes, analysis of Balzac's novella *Sarrasine* using a deconstructive procedure, and pointed out that all that Barthes was doing was replacing one narrative by another: 'To deconstruct a text is in a way a contradiction, since to deconstruct it is to make another construction out of the pieces.'[360] One is reminded of the point made by Professor Morris Zapp in David Lodge's *Small World*: that 'every decoding is another encoding'.[361]

An aspect of almost all the Nobel Lectures apart from those here cited, and which must have implications for would-be laureates in the practice of writing, is the sheer absence of any mention of the vocabulary of critical theory. The process of creative writing is intuitive rather than analytical and structural. Perhaps Nadine Gordimer expressed the point most vividly in her Nobel Lecture: 'Writers themselves don't analyze what they do; to analyze would be to look down while crossing a canyon on a tightrope.'[362]

Fallen by the Wayside

Also Rans

Many of the writers who were considered for the prize for several years but ultimately rejected have been mentioned already in this book. The Nobel database reveals some other famous names which were proposed but eventually passed over.

During the period covered by the official Nobel Prize database (1901–50) the vast majority of the authors named will be completely unknown to most readers, certainly to those who are familiar only with the major Western languages. It is to be hoped that they are remembered fondly at least, and with a little respect, if they are lucky, in their countries of origin. They must have been rated highly in their day of course. Then there are also the very famous, all-too-familiar names, the really great names, which, though we all recognize them as such today, did not pass muster with the Nobel Committee in their day. With a shake of the head one wonders how the committee failed to recognize them as standing head and shoulders above their contemporaries. And many of these names recur several times: someone, somewhere loved them and was determined to make the committee perceive their greatness. Thus in the first decade or so of the award one finds among the nominees the names of Zola, Tolstoy, Ibsen, Swinburne, George Meredith, Thomas Hardy and Henry James. Hardy's name recurs during the twenties too, where one can find nominated such luminaries as the brilliant Austrian lyric poet, and collaborator with Richard Strauss, Hugo von Hofmannsthal, as well as H.G. Wells, the Viennese satirist Karl Kraus and Thornton Wilder. Nominated in the thirties were Theodore Dreiser, Erich Maria Remarque, Max Beerbohm, John Masefield, and in 1936 Sigmund Freud (to whom we shall return shortly). 1938 found Aldous Huxley competing with Margaret Mitchell, and in 1946 E.M. Forster was up against Franz Werfel. Finally, 1950 seems to have been a bumper year: Hermann Broch, Karl Jaspers, Graham Greene and Robert Graves among others.

There are also several surprises to be found in this period: the first Chinese nominee, Lin Yutang in 1940; a nomination for the Iranian writer Abol-Gassem E'tessam Zadeh in 1944 and the first Egyptian nominee, Taha Hussein, in 1949. The honour of the most-nominated writer and therefore the most frequently passed-over writer during this period goes to Johannes V. Jensen, the Danish author, for whom one can find fifty-three nominations in the database. He was finally awarded the prize in 1944. Coming in second was the Spanish writer, Angel Guimerà y Jorge, born in The Canary Islands, and later living in Catalonia, and for whom there were twenty-one nominations, but who was never awarded the prize.

Freud's case is an interesting one. He was of course a scientist and not a literary figure, but he was admired by many for his impressive mastery of German prose style (he was in fact awarded the coveted Goethe Prize, for good style in scientific writing). He was nominated in 1936 by his friend and Nobel laureate Romain Rolland [1915]. There is clear evidence in the Nobel committee's reports however, that they were very antipathetic to Freud's theories of psychoanalysis, and regarded him as a corruptor of literature.[363] And on several occasions Per Hallström revealed his animosity in the context of award ceremony speeches. In his speech for the award to Pirandello in 1934 he was critical of the psychological concept of complexes, and expressed the belief that the writings of Pirandello could save people from entrapment in such ideas: 'He warns us not to touch the delicate tissue of the human soul in a coarsely dogmatic and blind manner.'[364] In his speech for Eugene O'Neill, in 1936, he said of *Mourning Becomes Electra*, that it was partly based 'upon the Freudian omniscience concerning the unconscious' and added 'These hypotheses are not, as we know, established beyond dispute.'[365]

Since 1950 there have been many rumours, but, due to the fifty-year rule, few of them can be verified, except by scholars with a knowledge of Swedish. Now and again some apparently reliable information comes to light. Thus earlier this year, 2012, a fascinating report appeared in the British newspaper, *The Guardian* (Thursday, 5th January 2012). The journalist, Alison Flood had studied, it appears, an article by the Swedish journalist Andreas Ekström, published in the Swedish newspaper *Sydsvenska Dagbladet*. The Swedish journalist had been delving into the recently opened Nobel archives for 1961, previously unavailable. The actual winner in 1961 was Ivo Andrić, from the former Yugoslavia, and who wrote in Serbo-Croatian. According to Flood, the poet Robert Frost was passed over because of his advanced age as was E.M. Forster, though, as she points out, this did not stop the Academy from awarding the prize to Doris Lessing at a sprightly eighty-seven in 2007. Lawrence Durrell was dismissed because of his obsession with eroticism, and Alberto Moravia was regarded as quite simply monotonous. Apparently Graham Greene's highest achievement was as second choice, with Karen Blixen was allowed only a third place. It seems that the Swedish journalist had been conducting this research over the previous five years, and pointed out that at that time there were about 300 proposals every year. What caught Flood's attention especially, was the fact that one author who had established a worldwide reputation, not least through the highly successful films based on his works, was rather summarily dismissed. It seems that for Anders Österling, the prose of J.R.R. Tolkien's trilogy *The Lord of the Rings* 'has not in any way measured up to storytelling of the highest quality'.[366]

Whatever happened to.....Pontoppidan?

Do you really want people to be asking a question like that of your name in a century from now? Or worse still to be asking something like: Pontoppidan? What's that? Isn't it some kind of unleavened bread?

It is bad enough to be nominated once or even several times and then be rejected, but to win, gain all the glory and admiration, and then ultimately to be completely forgotten, except amongst literary historians and in your own small neck of the woods, is not that a fate worse than never having been recognized as a writer at all?

Be honest, have you, or has indeed anyone of your acquaintance, ever read a work by Bjørnstjerne Bjørnson [1903], Paul Heyse [1910], Władysław Stanisław Reymont [1924], not to mention any by Sillenpää [1939], Laxness [1955], or Jiménez [1956]? And what of that elusive pair Eyvind Johnson and Harry Martinson, who shared the prize in 1974? You would also be hard pushed to find copies of works by Anatole France and Romain Rolland in your local library, let alone in a certain extensive chain of high-street bookstores, the 'Touchstones' of popular taste.

So what of Henrik Pontoppidan? Was he really able to sell books with a name like that? In his favour it must be said that he did not like his family name much himself. It derives apparently from the Danish name 'Broby' which translates as 'Bridge by the City'. But in the seventeenth century educated Danes developed the habit of latinizing their names. Thus 'Bridge by the City' ('pons oppidum') became Pontoppidan.[367] So much for quirky names. It seems that it might be worthwhile taking a look at some of his writing again, which is praised in the Nobel citation for its 'authentic descriptions of present-day life in Denmark',[368] if you can still find some of his works in translation. But would they still have a more universal appeal? It prompts one to wonder if it is not time to found a special society to revive interest in long neglected authors and creative people in general, which might be dubbed 'The Foundation for Forgotten and Undervalued Creativity' (FFFUC).

Thus, finally, our would-be laureate must ask him – or herself – very seriously, if, on achieving that impossible dream, whether they could live with the eventual likely loss of that fame, with being consigned to the more obscure corners of the Nobel Prize database?

If you are on the verge of giving up all hope, there is one more option that might appeal.

The Strindberg Option

C.D. af Wirsén dominated the award process for the Nobel Prize in Literature for about three decades in the early years. He was not only the Permanent Secretary of the Swedish Academy but also an influential critic writing in *Posttidningen*. Novelty and experimentation had little chance of gaining favour on his watch. Espmark describes him as 'the implacable opponent of the new directions in Swedish and Scandinavian literature'.[369] One influential and greatly admired Swedish writer never had a hope in hell: August Strindberg. But he was also never formally proposed, which reflects the conservatism prevailing in society as a whole at the time.

There was some rumour of his receiving the prize in 1909, when it in fact went to its first woman as well as its first Swede: Selma Lagerlöf. Many supporters of Strindberg were furious, and the Social Democratic Youth Alliance started a campaign to raise money for a special award for his literary achievement. Several prominent persons made contributions, including Nathan Söderblom, a prominent theologian, and well-known as an architect of the ecumenical movement in the twentieth century. From 1894 to 1901, by one of those little quirks of history, he was in Paris, where at that time both Alfred Nobel and August Strindberg were in his congregation. In 1930 he was awarded the Nobel Peace Prize. The majority of the 20,000 donors were workers, and finally they were able to collect about 45,000 kronor.[370]

In the light of these machinations on Strindberg's behalf, it is tempting to perceive a degree of personal resentment and indeed sour grapes in Strindberg's essay of 1910, 'Address to the Swedish Nation', in which he criticized bitterly the very first award to Prudhomme. His comments focused on the issue discussed in the first chapter of the present book: how one should interpret the Swedish word 'idealisk' as used by Nobel in his will. Sture Allén analysed Strindberg's critique in his own essay, 'Topping Shakespeare? Aspects of the Nobel Prize for [sic] Literature', included on the Nobel Prize website. Allén quotes Strindberg's final judgement that the award to Prudhomme had been made 'contrary to statutes and will'.[371] It other words, Strindberg believed that the committee had got it all wrong from the very start.

A lesson for would-be laureates has thus been around since the early days of the award: if no one qualified to do so will propose you, persuade your friends to set up a special prize in your name and for you alone, and have them pass the hat round to all who are willing to contribute. In that way you can obtain some compensation for the loss of the monetary aspect of the Nobel Prize, and reassure yourself that the mere mention of your name is enough to summon up massive support. You might even get away with calling it 'The Noble Prize *For* Literature'.

Select Bibliography

Online sources

All award ceremony speeches (Presentation Speeches), Banquet Speeches and Nobel Lectures, together with official short biographies, bibliographies, and also audio and video recordings of some speeches, together with other information available on some authors can be accessed through the official Nobel website, at nobelprize.org. Also accessible on this site are the following essays on aspects of the Nobel Prize in Literature:

Allén, Sture, 'Topping Shakespeare? Aspects of the Nobel Prize for Literature.'

Espmark, Kjell, 'The Nobel Prize in Literature'.

Svensén, Bo, 'The Nobel Prize in Literature: Nominations and Reports 1901–1950'.

Books

Espmark, Kjell, *The Nobel Prize in Literature, A Study of the Criteria behind the Choices*, G.K. Hall & Co., Boston, Massachusetts, USA, 1991

Lovell, Julia, *The Politics of Cultural Capital: China's Quest for a Nobel Prize in Literature*, University of Hawaii Press, Honolulu, 2006

Österling, Anders, 'The Literary Prize', in *Nobel: The Man and His Prizes*, Stockholm, 1972, (1950).

Sutherland, John, (Introduction) *Nobel Lectures. 20 years of the Nobel Prize for Literature Lectures*, Icon Books, Cambridge, UK, 2007.

Other works referred to

de Beauvoir, Simone, *Adieux: A Farewell to Sartre*, Penguin, London, 1985

Lodge, David, *Small World*, Secker and Warberg, 1984.

List of Nobel Laureates in Literature

The list is chronological, with information provided on the author's nationality and/or prime country of abode at the time of the award and the language(s) he or she wrote/writes in, together with occasional notes on other significant aspects of the award. Space is left at the end for the reader to update the list over the next decade, should the reader and books in general last that long. The information was retrieved from the official website of the Nobel Prize and other sources.

Year	Name	Country	Language
1901	Sully Prudhomme	France	French
1902	Theodor Mommsen	Germany	German
1903	Bjørnstjerne Bjørnson	Norway	Norwegian
1904	Frédéric Mistral &	France	French
	José Echegaray	Spain	Spanish
1905	Henryk Sienkiewicz	Poland	Polish
1906	Giosuè Carducci	Italy	Italian
1907	Rudyard Kipling	Great Britain	English
1908	Rudolf Eucken	Germany	German
1909	Selma Lagerlöf	Sweden	Swedish
1910	Paul Heyse	Germany	German
1911	Maurice Maeterlinck	Belgium	French
1912	Gerhart Hauptmann	Germany	German
1913	Rabindranath Tagore	India	Bengali & English
1914	*Prize reserved*		
1915	*Prize reserved*		
1916	Romain Rolland	France	French
	(for 1915)		
	Verner von Heidenstam	Sweden	Swedish
	(for 1916)		
1917	Karl Gjellerup &	Denmark	Danish
	Henrik Pontoppidan	Denmark	Danish
1918	*Prize reserved*		
1919	*Prize reserved*		
1920	Carl Spitteler *(for 1919)*	Switzerland	German
	Knut Hamsun *(for 1920)*	Norway	Norwegian
1921	Anatole France	France	French
1922	Jacinto Benavente	Spain	Spanish

1923	William Butler Yeats	Ireland	English
1924	Władysław Stanisław Reymont	Poland	Polish
1925	*Prize reserved*		
1926	George Bernard Shaw *(for 1925)*	Ireland	English
	Prize for 1926 reserved		
1927	Grazia Deledda *(for 1926)*	Italy	Italian
	Prize for 1927 reserved		
1928	Henri Bergson *(for 1927)*	France	French
	Sigrid Undset *(for 1928)*	Norway	Norwegian
1929	Thomas Mann	Germany	German
1930	Sinclair Lewis	United States	English
1931	Erik Axel Karlfeldt *(posthumously)*	Sweden	Swedish
1932	John Galsworthy	Great Britain	English
1933	Ivan Bunin	France (born in Russia)	Russian
1934	Luigi Pirandello	Italy	Italian
1935	*Prize reserved*		
1936	Eugene O'Neill	United States	English
1937	Roger Martin du Gard	France	French
1938	Pearl Buck	United States	English
1939	Frans Eemil Sillanpää	Finland	Finnish
1940–43	*No awards made*		
1944	Johannes V. Jensen	Denmark	Danish
1945	Gabriela Mistral	Chile	Spanish
1946	Hermann Hesse	Switzerland	German
1947	André Gide	France	French
1948	T.S. Eliot	Great Britain	English
1949	*Prize reserved*		
1950	William Faulkner *(for 1949)*	United States	English
	Bertrand Russell *(for 1950)*	Great Britain	English
1951	Pär Lagerkvist	Sweden	Swedish
1952	François Mauriac	France	French
1953	Winston Churchill	Great Britain	English
1954	Ernest Hemingway	United States	English
1955	Halldór Kiljan Laxness	Iceland	Icelandic
1956	Juan Ramón Jiménez	Spain	Spanish
1957	Albert Camus	France	French
1958	Boris Pasternak *(accepted but forced to decline)*	Soviet Union	Russian
1959	Salvatore Quasimodo	Italy	Italian

1960	Saint-John Perse	France	French
1961	Ivo Andrić	Yugoslavia	Serbo-Croatian
1962	John Steinbeck	United States	English
1963	Giorgos Seferis	Greece	Greek
1964	Jean-Paul Sartre (*declined the award*)	France	French
1965	Mikhail Sholokhov	Soviet Union	Russian
1966	Shmuel Yosef Agnon &	Israel	Hebrew
	Nelly Sachs	Germany (living in Sweden)	German
1967	Miguel Ángel Asturias	Guatemala	Spanish
1968	Yasunari Kawabata	Japan	Japanese
1969	Samuel Beckett	Ireland	English & French
1970	Aleksandr Solzhenitsyn	Soviet Union	Russian
1971	Pablo Neruda	Chile	Spanish
1972	Heinrich Böll	Germany (Federal Republic)	German
1973	Patrick White	Australia	English
1974	Eyvind Johnson &	Sweden	Swedish
	Harry Martinson	Sweden	Swedish
1975	Eugenio Montale	Italy	Italian
1976	Saul Bellow	United States	English
1977	Vicente Aleixandre	Spain	Spanish
1978	Isaac Bashevis Singer	United States (born in Poland)	Yiddish
1979	Odysseus Elytis	Greece	Greek
1980	Czesław Miłosz	United States & Poland	Polish
1981	Elias Canetti	Great Britain (born in Bulgaria)	German
1982	Gabriel García Márquez	Colombia	Spanish
1983	William Golding	Great Britain	English
1984	Jaroslav Seifert	Czechoslovakia	Czech
1985	Claude Simon	France	French
1986	Wole Soyinka	Nigeria	English
1987	Joseph Brodsky	United States (born in Russia)	Russian & English
1988	Naguib Mahfouz	Egypt	Arabic
1989	Camilo José Cela	Spain	Spanish
1990	Octavio Paz	Mexico	Spanish
1991	Nadine Gordimer	South Africa	English
1992	Derek Walcott	Saint Lucia	English

1993	Toni Morrison	United States	English
1994	Kenzaburō Ōe	Japan	Japanese
1995	Seamus Heaney	Ireland	English
1996	Wisława Szymborska	Poland	Polish
1997	Dario Fo	Italy	Italian
1998	José Saramago	Portugal	Portuguese
1999	Günter Grass	Germany	German
2000	Gao Xingjian	France (born in P.R. of China)	Chinese
2001	V.S. Naipaul	Great Britain	English
2002	Imre Kertész	Hungary	Hungarian
2003	J.M. Coetzee	South Africa	English
2004	Elfriede Jelinek	Austria	German
2005	Harold Pinter	Great Britain	English
2006	Orhan Pamuk	Turkey	Turkish
2007	Doris Lessing	Great Britain	English
2008	J.M.G. Le Clézio	France & Mauritius	French
2009	Herta Müller	Germany (born in Romania)	German
2010	Mario Vargas Llosa	Peru & Spain	Spanish
2011	Tomas Tranströmer	Sweden	Swedish
2012			
2013			
2014			
2015			
2016			
2017			
2018			
2019			
2020			
2021			
2022			

Notes

To save space, all references to the official Nobel Prize website are only partial. In each case the reference begins with a forward slash. The reference should be preceded by:www.nobelprize.org in each case. References to all other websites are written in full.

1. /alfred_nobel/will/will-full
2. ibid
3. /nobel_prizes/literature/articles/sture
4. ibid
5. ibid
6. ibid
7. /alfred_nobel/will/will-full
8. ibid
9. /nobel_organisations/nobelfoundation/statutes, §2
10. /nobel_prizes/literature/articles/espmark
11. /nobel_prizes/literature/laureates/1901
12. /nobel_organisations/nobelfoundation/statutes, §2
13. /nobel_prizes/literature/laureates/1902
14. /nobel_prizes/literature/laureates/1903
15. /nobel_organisations/nobelfoundation/statutes, §7 and §8
16. /nobel_prizes/literature/laureates/1964
17. ibid
18. ibid
19. ibid
20. ibid
21. ibid
22. de Beauvoir, p. 242
23. ibid p. 246
24. ibid p. 247
25. ibid p. 248
26. ibid pp. 252–53
27. ibid p. 253
28. ibid
29. ibid p. 242
30. /nobel_prizes/literature/laureates/1958
31. ibid
32. www.frerl.org/articleprintview/1496794
33. www.washingtonpost.com/wp-dyn/content/article/2007/01/26
34. www.frerl.org/articleprintview/1496794

35. Quoted from Feltrinelli, C, *Senior Service: The Life of Giangiacomo Feltrinelli*, Moscow, 2003, p. 131

36. ibid p. 122

37. Sergeyeva-Klyatis, Anna, 'International Provocation: On Boris Pasternak's Nobel Prize', in Social Sciences, No. 3, 2011, pp. 44–57, Moscow

38. Tolstoy, I, *The Laundered Nobel: Boris Pasternak's* Doctor Zhivago *Between the KGB and the CIA*, Moscow, 2009, p. 7

39. Quoted in Sergeyeva-Klyatis, Anna, p. 7. See note 37 for details.

40. english.pravda.ru / society / showbiz / 18.-12-2003-pasternak

41. ibid

42. ibid

43. Espmark, p. 101

44. / nobel_prizes / literature / laureates / 1933

45. ibid

46. ibid

47 ibid

48. Espmark, p. 62

49. ibid

50. ibid pp. 62–63

51. ibid

52. ibid

53 ibid

54. ibid

55. ibid

56. Espmark, p. 99

57. ibid p. 100

58. ibid p. 100

59. ibid p. 111

60. ibid pp. 106–7

61. / nobel_prizes / literature / laureates / 1965

62. ibid

63. ibid

64. ibid

65. ibid

66. ibid

67. ibid

68. / nobel_prizes / literature / laureates / 1970

69. Espmark p. 82

70. ibid pp. 100–1

71. ibid p. 112

72. ibid

73. ibid

74. ibid p. 113

75. /nobel_prizes/literature/laureates/1970/Solzhenitsyn-article
76. ibid
77. ibid
78. ibid
79. ibid
80. ibid
81. /nobel_prizes/literature/laureates/1970
82. ibid
83. ibid
84. ibid
85. ibid
86. ibid
87. Espmark p. 119
88. /nobel_prizes/literature/laureates/1987
89. ibid
90. ibid
91. ibid
92. ibid
93. /nobel_prizes/literature/laureates/1905
94. ibid
95. Espmark p. 93
96. /nobel_prizes/literature/laureates/1961
97. ibid
98. /nobel_prizes/literature/laureates/1984
99. ibid
100. ibid
101. Espmark p. 118
102. /nobel_prizes/literature/laureates/1980
103. ibid
104. ibid
105. Espmark p. 116
106. ibid
107. ibid p. 117
108. /nobel_prizes/literature/laureates/1972
109. Translations from Böll's Banquet Speech are by the present author.
110. /nobel_prizes/literature/laureates/1972
111. ibid
112. ibid
113. ibid
114. ibid
115. ibid
116. /nobel_prizes/literature/laureates/1959
117. ibid

118. /nobel_prizes/literature/laureates/1980
119. /nobel_prizes/literature/laureates/1960
120. ibid
121. ibid
122. ibid
123. /nobel_prizes/literature/laureates/1966
124. ibid
125. /nobel_prizes/literature/laureates/1967
126. ibid
127. ibid
128. /nobel_prizes/literature/laureates/2000
129. ibid
130. ibid
131. Jaggi, Maya, *The Guardian*, Saturday, 2nd August 2008
132. Lovell p. 171
133. ibid p. 172
134. ibid p. 173
135. ibid p. 174
136. ibid
137. ibid p. 189 note 13
138. /nobel_prizes/literature/laureates/1923
139. ibid
140. ibid
141. ibid
142. ibid
143. /nobel_prizes/literature/laureates/1995
144. ibid
145. /nobel_prize/literature/laureates/1955
146. ibid
147. Espmark, p. 107
148. ibid
149. ibid
150. ibid
151. /nobel_prizes/literature/laureates/1939
152. ibid
153. ibid
154. Espmark p. 103
155. ibid p. 104
156. /nobel_prizes/literature/laureates/1948
157. /nobel_prizes/literature/laureates/1902
158. ibid
159. ibid
160. Espmark p. 147

161. ibid p. 105
162. ibid p. 106
163. ibid
164. /nobel_prizes/literature/laureates/1953
165. ibid
166. ibid
167. /nobel_prizes/literature/laureates/1908
168. ibid
169. Espmark p. 9
170. ibid p. 90
171. /nobel_prizes/literature/laureates/1908
172. ibid note
173. Österling p. 110
174. Espmark p. 165
175. /nobel_prizes/literature/laureates/1927
176. ibid
177. ibid
178. /nobel_prizes/literature/laureates/1950
179. ibid
180. ibid
181. ibid
182. /nobel_prizes/literature/laureates/1904
183. ibid
184. ibid
185. ibid
186. Espmark p. 19
187. ibid
188. ibid
189. ibid p. 27
190. /nobel_prizes/literature/laureates/1912
191. Espmark p. 41
192. ibid
193. ibid
194. /nobel_prizes/literature/laureates/1922
195. ibid
196. ibid
197. /nobel_prizes/literature/laureates/1922
198. Espmark p. 25
199. Espmark p. 47
200. /nobel_prizes/literature/laureates/1925
201. Espmark p. 150
202. /nobel_prizes/literature/laureates/1934
203. ibid

204. ibid
205. Espmark p. 69
206. ibid
207. /nobel_prizes/literature/laureates/1936
208. ibid
209. ibid
210. ibid
211. Epsmark p. 82
212. /nobel_prizes/literature/laureates/1969
213. ibid
214. ibid
215. /nobel_prizes/literature/laureates/1986
216. ibid
217. ibid
218. ibid
219. ibid
220. /nobel_prizes/literature/laureates/2005
221. ibid
222. ibid
223. ibid
224. /nobel_prizes/literature/laureates/1971
225. /nobel_prizes/literature/laureates/1960
226. ibid
227. /nobel_prizes/literature/laureates/1913
228. ibid
229. ibid
230. Espmark p. 58
231. /Nobel_prizes/literature/laureates/1931
232. ibid
233. /nobel_prizes/literature/laureates/1948
234. ibid
235. /nobel_prizes/literature/laureates/1959
236. ibid
237. /nobel_prizes/literature/laureates/1963
238. ibid
239. Espmark p. 59
240. ibid p. 132
241. ibid p. 139
242. /nobel_prizes/literature/laureates/1968
243. /nobel_prizes/literature/laureates/1996
244. ibid
245. /nobel_prizes/literature/laureates/2004
246. ibid

247. Espmark p. 147
248. /nobel_prizes/literature/laureates/1910
249. Espmark p. 33
250. /nobel_prizes/literature/laureates/1920
251. ibid
252. Espmark p. 40
253. /nobel_prizes/literature/laureates/1921
254. Espmark p. 50
255. /nobel_prizes/literature/laureates/ 1928
256. Espmark p. 52
257. /nobel_prizes/literature/laureates/1929
258. /nobel_prizes/literature/laureates/1930
259. ibid
260. /nobel_prizes/literature/laureates/ 1932
261. Espmark p. 63
262. /nobel_prizes/literature/laureates/1937
263. ibid
264. Espmark pp. 64–65
265. ibid
266. /nobel_prizes/literature/laureates/1938
267. ibid
268. Espmark p. 71
269. /nobel_prizes/literature/laureates/1947
270. ibid
271. /nobel_prizes/literature/laureates/ 1949
272. /nobel_prizes/literature/laurestes/1951
273. ibid
274. ibid
275. /nobel_prizes/literature/laureates/1952
276. ibid
277. Espmark p. 106
278. ibid p. 105
279. /nobel_prizes/literature/laureates/1954
280. ibid
281. /nobel_prizes/literature/laureates/1957
282. ibid
283. /nobel_prizes/literature/laureates/1967
284. ibid
285. Espmark p. 116
286. /nobel_prizes/literature/laureates/1972
287. /nobel_prizes/literature/laureates/1973
288. ibid
289. /nobel_prizes/literature/laureates/1976

290. ibid
291. ibid
292. /nobel_prizes/literature/laureates/1981
293. ibid
294. ibid. (Translation from the German by the present writer)
295. /nobel_prizes/literature/laureates/1982
296. ibid
297. ibid
298. /nobel_prizes/literature/laureates/1983
299. ibid
300. /nobel_prizes/literature/laureates/1985
301. ibid
302. ibid
303. /nobel_prizes/literature/laureates/1988
304. ibid
305. /nobel_prizes/literature/laureates/1991
306. ibid
307. /nobel_prizes/literature/laureates/1993
308. ibid
309. ibid
310. /nobel_prizes/literature/laureates/1994
311. ibid
312. /nobel_prizes/literature/laureates/1999
313. ibid
314. /nobel_prizes/literature/laureates/2001
315. ibid
316. /nobel_prizes/literature/laureates/2003
317. /nobel_prizes/literature/laureates/2004
318. http://news.bbc.co.uk/go/pr/fr-/2/hi/entertainment
319. /nobel_prizes/literature/laureates/2006
320. ibid
321. ibid
322. ibid
323. ibid
324. /nobel_prizes/literature/laureates/2006
325. /nobel_prizes/literature/laureates/2007
326. ibid
327. ibid
328. ibid
329. /nobel_prizes/literature/laureates/2007
330. /nobel_prizes/literature/laureates/2008
331. ibid
332. ibid

333. ibid
334. /nobel_prizes/literature/laureates/2009
335. ibid
336. ibid
337. /nobel_prizes/literature/laureates/2010
338. ibid
339. ibid
340. /nobel_prizes/literature/laureates/1919
341. Espmark pp. 31 and 123
342. ibid p. 29
343. ibid p. 31
344. ibid
345. ibid p. 36
346. ibid
347. /nobel_prizes/literature/laureates/1919
348. /nobel_prizes/peace/laureates/1935
349. /nobel_prizes/literature/laureates/1997
350. /nobel_prizes/literature/laureates/1949
351. /nobel_prizes/literature/laureates/1972
352. /nobel_prizes/literature/laureates/1967
353. /nobel_prizes/literature/laureates/1986
354. /nobel_prizes/literature/laureates/1999
355. ibid
356. /nobel_prizes/literature/laureates/1938
357. ibid
358. /nobel_prizes/literature/laureates/1983
359. /nobel_prizes/literature/laureates/1990
360. /nobel_prizes/literature/laureates/1991
361. Lodge, p. 25
362. /nobel_prizes/literature/laureates/1991
363. Epsmark, p. 67
364. /nobel_prizes/literature/laureates/1934
365. /nobel_prizes/literature/laureates/1936
366. In *The Guardian*, Thursday 5th January 2012
367. See www.e-poke.dk/pontoppidan_bio_01.asp in Danish
368. /nobel_prizes/literature/laureates/1917
369. Espmark, p. 10
370. See also Meyer, Michael, *Strindberg: A Biography*, Oxford, 1987.
371. /nobel_prizes/literature/articles/sture

Biographical note

Dr David Carter has taught at St Andrews and Southampton universities in the UK and has been Professor of Communicative English at Yonsei University, Seoul. His Ph.D. was on Freud's theories of creativity and aesthetics and he has taught on Freud and Jung, and also on the German Romantics, the brothers Grimm and the 'Märchen' tradition. He has published on psychoanalysis, literature, drama, film history and applied linguistics, is also a freelance journalist and translator, and has published books on the Belgian author Georges Simenon and Literary Theory, as well as in the field of film studies, the most recent being *East Asian Cinema* and *The Western*. For Hesperus he has written *Brief Lives: Honoré de Balzac*, *Brief Lives: Sigmund Freud* and *Brief Lives: Marquis de Sade*. He has also translated Balzac's 'Sarrasine', Georges Simenon's *Three Crimes*, Klaus Mann's *Alexander* and Sigmund Freud *On Cocaine*, and other works.

HESPERUS PRESS

Hesperus Press is committed to bringing near what is far –
far both in space and time. Works written by the greatest
authors, and unjustly neglected or simply little known in
the English-speaking world, are made accessible through
new translations and a completely fresh editorial approach.
Through these classic works, the reader is introduced to the
greatest writers from all times and all cultures.

For more information on Hesperus Press, please visit our
website: **www.hesperuspress.com**